SEX MAKES THE WORLD GO ROUND

SEX MAKES THE WORLD GO ROUND

Colette Chiland

Translated by David Alcorn and
Philip Slotkin (Chapter 1)

KARNAC

First published in 2008 by
Karnac Books Ltd
118 Finchley Road, London NW3 5HT

British Library Cataloguing in Publication Data
A C.I.P for this book is available from the British Library

ISBN-13: 978-1-85575-546-8

Typeset, designed and produced by
Florence Production Ltd, Stoodleigh, Devon
www.florenceproduction.co.uk

Printed and bound in Great Britain by
Biddles Ltd., King's Lynn, Norfolk

www.karnacbooks.com

CONTENTS

ABOUT THE AUTHOR

Collette Chiland read philosophy and psychology, then medicine and psychiatry at the University of Paris. She taught clinical psycology at La Sorbonne, then at Université Paris Descartes, and is training analyst at the Paris Psychoanalytical Society. She was psychiatrist-in-chief at the Alfred-Binet, and is Honorary President of the International Association for Child and Adolescent Psychiatry and Allied Professions.

PREFACE

The idea of writing this book came to me as a result of the many themes that over time had caught my attention. I had for several years taught a seminar on the topic of women, the modern world and psychoanalysis. I do not intend here to discuss in any depth Freud and the post-Freudians; I shall simply refer to some of Freud's points of view.

I was also researching the topic of sex differences in psycho-pathology: more boys than girls are taken to be examined by a child psychiatrist; boys are more vulnerable than girls in their psycho-biological development; on average, men die younger than women. In other words, the weaker of the two sexes is in fact the male one, even though women—Simone de Beauvoir's famous "second sex"—are treated as being inferior.

I had long been familiar with Robert Jesse Stoller's work, about which I recently published a book (Chiland, 2003a), when, one day, a 4-year-old boy entered my consulting-room; he looked exactly like the description that Stoller makes of what he used to call in the 1960s "a transsexual boy". That was my first encounter with trans-sexualism; I was later to spend several years working in a Gender Identity Clinic.

That work made me think again and from a different perspective about masculinity and femininity and encouraged me to write two books, published originally in French then in English translation: *Transsexualism: Illusion and Reality* (Chiland, 2003b) and *Exploring Transsexualism* (Chiland, 2005).

The present book is a further development of my thinking on sexuality and gender identity. Before training as a physician and psychoanalyst, I had studied philosophy: I tend therefore to integrate what I learn from clinical practice into the way I think about humanity in general; when I do this, however, I strive to avoid any "jargonizing". I am thus very much part of the French tradition in that philosophical concerns are always present in my mind, but at the same time I stand back somewhat from that tradition in that as far as possible I use ordinary words to express my ideas.

Naturally enough, this book contains several references both to English texts and to French writers; since not all of the latter have been translated into English, the ideas developed in them may well be unfamiliar to the English-speaking world. The anglophone reader may at times feel disoriented. France is not bathed in the same cultural light as are Britain and America. The fact that some texts referred to have not been translated into English is not the main point: what is uppermost is the difference in cultural atmosphere.

In France, persecution of homosexuals has never reached the kind of heights that the United States has had to contend with, for example, or Britain for that matter. No candidate for employment has ever in France been asked about his or her sexual orientation. There has never been the kind of puritanism that gave rise to laws prohibiting anal intercourse, nor have legal proceedings been taken against any man for wanting to have intercourse with his wife three times a week . . . and so on. As a result, it is still possible, in France, to ask questions and to discuss issues that have become more or less taboo in the United States. I am not homophobic, but neither am I "heterophobic", as is the case in some feminist quarters where heterosexuality is thought of as leading to the enslavement of women and to forced procreation.

There are two main themes which run through the whole of this book. The first is the distinction, established by Freud and based on clinical data, between the two currents of sexuality: tenderness and sensuality. For sexuality to be complete, both of these currents have to be combined. Some people challenge the merit of the distinction drawn by Freud. It is nonetheless a leitmotif in his writings that seems to have gone largely unnoticed. I, however, have found it extremely helpful in trying to disentangle the various issues involved in what I call "sexual wanderings"—the sexual quest that plagues human beings and leads some of them to perversion, pornography or prostitution. Tenderness is reduced almost to the point of disappearing altogether, leaving the way clear for sensuality alone.

It is at this point that the other main theme of this book appears: women have always been treated as inferior beings. They have always lost out whenever sexual wanderings have been uppermost. It is only in the past two hundred years that a feminist movement has emerged in the West; thanks to that movement, women are much more liberated than before and their overall status has undoubtedly improved.

The paths an individual follows in choosing his or her object are always specific to the person involved, whether that object be of the same or of the opposite sex. To use John Money's well-chosen term, every one of us has a "lovemap", a combination of biological factors and life experiences that define the conditions under which any given individual will be able to experience pleasure. Why do some people think that, when we evoke the "psychological bedrock" which, derived from the child's earliest interactions with the environment, marks him or her for life, we are out to make the person involved feel guilty? Why do they think that only biological considerations— the "biological bedrock"—should be taken into account in order for that person not to feel guilty?

It is well known that Freud laid great emphasis on sexual matters. In the years that followed, a distinction was drawn between sex and gender, and the idea of gender identity was introduced. Human beings do not spend every minute of their lives copulating—but at every minute of their lives their gender identity is present. *Sex makes the world go round* implies that sex is everywhere, provided that we take into account both sexuality and gender identity. Of course, as far as material reality is concerned, money and other economic factors also make the world go round.

To focus for a moment on sexuality, it is undoubtedly true to say that it does play a major role in the lives of human beings. It ensures reproduction of the human species. However, in human beings, sexuality is dissociated from oestrus and from the reproductive process; it is infiltrated by ideology. In all societies, writes Maurice Godelier, one of the greatest of French anthropologists, sexuality is the echo chamber for all sorts of oppressive and exploitative relationships (Godelier, 1982, p. 353).

The struggle for equal rights should not make us forget the "sexual difference". Men and women *are* different—as to their genital organs, their psychosexual development, their position during intercourse, their roles in the reproductive process. Every society, however, interprets that fundamental difference in its own way— and that interpretation, of course, can and must be challenged.

I refer in this book to a distinction that is familiar to contemporary French philosophers involving three forms of love, expressed by the Greek words *Eros*, *Philia* and *Agapè*. I do so here in my own way, which is not that of other philosophers, because of the reference I make to sensuality and tenderness. In modern Greek, where it means simply "love", *Agapè* does not have the same religious connotation as it has in French. Although I have found it helpful to quote the apostle Paul, my overall perspective on this issue has nothing to do with religion as such. My intention is to make room for the moments when true love, acting selflessly and with egotistic sexual aims pushed aside, keeps destructive impulses firmly under control.

CHAPTER ONE

The heart of the matter[1]

As I write these lines in the year of grace 1998, no one can doubt that sex makes the world go round, for it is all-pervasive in the press, the broadcast media, and the Internet. One of the planet's leading politicians, President Bill Clinton of the United States, risked his public career for the sake of a private sexual affair. The barrier between the private and public domains has crumbled under the onslaught of a moralism that barely conceals the political interests lying behind it. The sexual antics of the great and famous as a rule occupy the minds only of "little people", who momentarily assume princely status by identifying with their joys and sorrows as reported in a sensationalist media that brings tears to the eyes of consumers of romantic pulp novelettes. This time, fact and fiction came together. The historical event mentioned above shows that the sexual appetite for seduction makes men throw caution and discretion to the winds. However, the subject-matter of my book transcends this consideration and concerns the personal life of every individual.

When I say that "*sex* makes the world go round", I am referring not only to *sexuality*—i.e., sexual relations—but also to *gender identity*, which denotes an individual's sense of belonging to one or other sex or gender. Rather than compile an encyclopaedia on the subject, I wish to discuss the *importance of sexuality and gender identity* in human life—for they are so important that sex may indeed be said to make the world go round.

Aside from schizogenesis in single-celled organisms, cloning, and parthenogenesis, all three of which result in the reproduction of an identical individual, life is perpetuated by innovative sexual procreation. Hence sex, life, and death are interconnected. Some organisms die in the process of mating, having seemingly lived through the stages of growth, metamorphosis from egg to larva or caterpillar, and then to butterfly or adult insect, solely in order to reproduce in a single act and to die. Others reproduce throughout their lives, but at certain times only.

Although human beings are not subject to oestrus and can have sexual intercourse outside the ovulation-related period of heat, there is still a "biological clock", for the menopause marks the end of the human female's reproductive capacity. Even if humans can come together at any time simply for pleasure, the complications of their psychic life have led them to invent ideological connections between sexuality and procreation. Liberated in their bodies, they remain the prisoners of their individual and collective representations, their personal fantasies, and their cultural myths. Human sexuality is always a *psychosexuality*, a source of abundant riches and of harsh vicissitudes alike.

Because our culture has developed the sense of individuality to an extent unparalleled in any other, the individual insists on the right to gratify his or her demand for pleasure, often at any price. Even though sexuality has become dissociated from procreation in many ways, it encounters prohibitions: since man is a *zôon politikón*—a social animal subject to the constraints of civilization—human beings must sacrifice some of their "savage" sexuality (the "sexual life of savages" is not the same as savage sexuality).

I wrote this book on the basis of my experience as a psychoanalyst, my meditation on the writings of Freud, and my reading in a variety of fields. Freud, of course, is one of those who did most to draw attention to the importance of sexuality, with the result that he has been—wrongly—accused of pansexualism, whereas it seems that many of the psychoanalysts who came after him have forgotten about the importance of sexuality (but see McDougall, 1995; Green, 1997). Nor, perhaps, have psychoanalysts written much about love (those who have include Person, 1989, and Kernberg, 1995).

Some seek to minimize or even to forget the fact that man is an animal. Man is admittedly a special animal, but an animal for all that:

the most gifted of animals in the spheres of mental representation, communication in language, toolmaking, and attempts to conceive of the universe as a whole, in terms of its origins, meaning, and purpose, as well as the invention of worlds beyond worlds. Man is also the most tortured of animals—a "denatured animal" in the words of Vercors (1952)—who has lost the capacity to experience the immediacy of satisfaction, and can rediscover how to live the instant to the full only through a spiritual, ascetic quest.

Even if human sexuality is a psychosexuality, it is nevertheless rooted in biological reality, as Freud was always aware. I disagree with Laplanche (1993) that Freud was guilty of a "biologizing sidetracking of sexuality". Following in the footsteps of others who have studied gender identity—a subject not tackled by Freud as such, given his concentration on sexuality—I (Chiland, 1997) came to realize the extent to which the ultimate foundation of all differences between the sexes is the *sexual difference*. By this I mean everything, based on the difference between the genital organs, that comes to govern the relations between the sexes: the experience of one's body, the sexual cycle, the position in intercourse, and the role in pro-creation. Every society imposes an interpretation of the sexual difference on the individual, defining female and male in such a way that it is quite hard work to identify the elements that cannot be obliterated or denied in the sexual difference.

A child's discovery that there are other human beings who are both like and unlike him- or herself, is a trauma that underlies such manifestations as castration anxiety and penis envy. To make this trauma bearable, humans feel a need for the support of a peer group, and one group tends to disparage the other in order to sustain the sense of its own worth. Men's disparagement of women has outweighed women's disparagement of men. Even if this has not always been so—who can say what the situation was in the beginning?—it is certainly the case throughout our present reality, giving rise to what Héritier (1996) calls the "differential valence of the sexes". This difference has always been interpreted as an inequality in women's disfavour, leading to their demeaning, subordination, and even ill-treatment. We may—indeed should—ask (yet we seldom do), why women put up for so long with this attribution of inferior status; why the "great revolution" (Abensour, 1921) of feminism took place only yesterday. If feminists neglect to pose this question in all its implications, it is because the idea that women might have internalized their devaluation is repugnant to them; not only men, but women themselves, need convincing of the absurdity of devaluing women.

The differences have indeed often been studied on the basis of the paradigm of man, *vir*, the male human being. As regards the genital organs, for a long time the female genitals were regarded as nothing but male organs turned inside out like the fingers of a glove (Laqueur, 1990). When it comes to sexuality, interest focuses on that of men; if homosexuality is proscribed, attention is directed to male homosexuality. Freud himself confined his studies to what happens in boys and men, extrapolating from the results to the situation in girls and women.

Some even deny the existence of any difference between men and women, as if "difference" were bound to be synonymous with "inequality". Whereas differences relate to the level of fact, equality and inequality are a matter of law. The struggle to secure equal rights for women is legitimate and can be waged without succumbing to the absurdity of disavowing all differences between the sexes or engaging in self-censorship on the grounds of political or sexual correctness.

However, the sexes not only confront each other but also seek each other out, for sexuality has two currents, a tender one and a sensual one. The vagaries of translation of the German word *zärtlich*—the only correct rendering is surely *tender*—have obscured the importance attached by Freud to these two aspects.

Every individual's erotic arousal is subject to demands of its own, and the origins of these "lovemaps" are difficult and sometimes impossible to determine. Can this arousal ever completely dissolve in sublimation? In a couple, it both binds the partners together and holds them apart, perhaps, as Stoller (1979) suggests, because of the hostility inherent within it. The capacity for intimacy presupposes overcoming the fear of interpenetration not only of bodies but also of souls.

Some individuals are turned on by the opposite sex and others by their own. Why are some people attracted exclusively to one sex while others have an insuperable aversion to it? Whereas it is not easy to explain homosexuality, is heterosexuality self-evidently the norm, as many would like to believe?

The exaltation of individual pleasure and the disparagement of the opposite sex lead to sexual wanderings in the form of perversion, prostitution, and pornography. What human needs do these cater to? Are they erotic forms of hate or hate-imbued forms of love?

The search for erotic gratification is not devoid of the wish to exert mastery over the other, just as there is no love without hate. Can ambivalence be neutralized—and overcome? There can be no love of the other without self-love, and self-love (healthy, happy narcissism) can arise only out of love for the other.

Love is *Eros*, *Philia*, and *Agapè*—three Greek words people like to use today to denote, respectively, the erotic search, friendship, and the selfless love invoked by Paul the Apostle in Corinthians 1, chapter 13. Without Agapè, in which Eros and Narcissus disappear, there may be sexuality, but can there be love?

Notes

1   Translated by Philip Slotkin MA (Cantab.) MITI

CHAPTER TWO

Freud and the importance of sexuality

Queen Victoria, whose name will always be evocative of an era of prudishness,[1] was still on the throne when, at the close of the 19th Century, Freud began treating patients and listening to what they had to say. Just a few years after she died (in 1901), Freud published his seminal work, *Three Essays on the Theory of Sexuality* (1905d)[2], which marked a turning point in his ideas on sexuality.

Freud had dreamt of a research career in neurophysiology, but at the time circumstances in Vienna made that option quite impossible. As a clinician, he would listen to his patients in a particularly attentive manner. Between 1890 and 1900, he published clinical papers that clearly show how his thinking was developing. The neurotic patients who came to him for treatment were suffering from a *psychic conflict*, and Freud gradually became convinced that sexuality was necessarily one of the poles of that conflict, whether it be the patient's *actual or infantile sexuality*. When he published his magnum opus, *Die Traumdeutung (The Interpretation of Dreams)* in 1900, Freud still believed that only neurotics have an infantile sexual life characterized by its precocity. However, in 1905, in his *Three Essays on the Theory of Sexuality*, he argued that infantile sexuality was in fact universal (manifestations of sexuality do not wait for puberty; as soon as they are born, children have a sexual life characterized by certain specific parameters), and he established a connection between infantile sexuality and perverse sexuality (the sexual life of children is not genital in nature, they do not have intercourse; their satisfaction is linked to other pleasurable zones [mouth, anus] that, in adults, are treated as pleasures preliminary to actual sexual union—or, if they are inflexibly and exclusively the focus of all their sexual activity, are called perverse).

Sexuality is always conflictual

In declaring that sexuality is all-important, Freud simultaneously defined the term in a much wider sense. For him, sexuality is present whatever a person's age, and begins as soon as the infant begins to suckle. That argument was sufficient for him to be accused of *pansexualism*. Yet at no point did Freud claim that the only factor to be taken into consideration was the sexual instinct. He argued simply that sexuality is one of the poles in a conflict that, when resolved, leads to mental health and well-being, and, when it perseveres, results in mental illness; thus, sexuality is one of the components that go to make up the psyche, the personality and mental disorder. As to *the other pole* in that conflict, Freud did have occasion to change the manner in which he described it.

Initially, Freud thought that this conflict—from which every human being suffers—took place mainly between the internal and external worlds. Although there was indeed an internal conflict between the sexual instinct and the ego (self-preservation) instincts, this internal conflict gave rise to an external one, because the sexual instinct (libido) brought the individual into conflict with group morals and civilized morality; the ego instincts required submission to the rules established by society. In an article written in 1908, "'Civilized' sexual morality and modern nervous illness" (Freud, 1908d), he developed this point of view. That paper stimulated Wilhelm Reich's thinking and led him to believe that, in their sex life, human beings were subjected to repression by society at large.

However, Freud soon came to argue that the conflict was fundamentally an internal one, and as such inevitable. He discovered that the libido—love—was not directed exclusively towards some external person; there exists a form of self-love that is quite normal. There is a conflict between narcissistic love, in which the ego is its own love-object, and object love, in which the ego loves another.

In the final development of his theory, the internal conflict becomes much more deep-rooted. The protagonists now are *Eros*, the sexual instinct that impels an organism to unite with another—the life instinct—and *Thanatos*, a negative and destructive force—the death instinct. The mythical quality of the manner in which Freud formulated this final version of his theory has often been criticized. Yet it does have the merit of encouraging us to go beyond clinical data as such and think about the human condition itself.

The libido

With his initial grounding in biology, Freud saw human beings as related to animals. What some have seen as a "biologizing side-tracking of sexuality" (Laplanche, 1993) is, to my mind, absolutely fundamental to his way of thinking. Every human being is an animal—a particular kind of animal, complicated, of course, but an animal nonetheless. It is true that human beings have the power of speech, and that their language is incomparably more sophisticated than any means of communication that animals possess—but it remains a fact that human beings are animals. They are born, they suffer, and they die. Nothing can be experienced in the mind that is not to some extent rooted in the body. Freud attempted to think about mental life and culture without resorting to transcendence, going as far as to ignore the fact that culture is handed down through our *social heritage* and not by *biological heredity*.

Like animals, human beings are driven by impersonal forces. Freud called them *Triebe*, instincts;[3] this is the word, he says, that is used in biology to refer to needs, *Bedürfnisse*. A group of French translators of Freud's writings thought it better to invent a neologism—*pulsion*—for *Trieb*, even though over the centuries classical literature and philosophy had rendered *Trieb* by the word *instinct*. This school of thought argued that, since Freud's under-standing of instinct was innovative, a new word had to be found to accommodate it; however, in the original German, Freud had not found it necessary to invent a neologism—he used a perfectly ordinary term of the German language. At the same time, it was argued that Freud made a distinction between the sex drive and physiological needs; if this distinction is felt to be imperative and helpful, by all means let us make it—but we cannot claim Freud's support for such a proposition. There can be no doubt whatsoever that, from the outset, the *Three Essays on the Theory of Sexuality* proposes to designate the sexual needs and instincts by the term *libido* as a counterpart to the term *hunger*, designating the need for nourishment and the instinct that drives us to search for food. Freud contrasts libido and hunger—the latter term being a shorthand way of designating the set of physiological instincts pertaining to self-preservation; when he refers (in other papers) to the poets, the contrast he makes is between love and hunger.

The instincts exert constant pressure and are conservative in nature. The sexual instinct has as its aim the preservation of the species. It leads to copulation, and hence to the possibility of procreation, even though the individual's only aim may be personal pleasure. In order to have intercourse, animals risk their lives. Preservation of individuals belongs to what Freud was later to designate by a more general term than hunger: the instinct of self-preservation or ego-instinct, in other words an egotistic instinct.

Since the libido exerts constant pressure, it is an active force. Freud equated activity with masculinity, and argued that the libido is essentially virile in nature.

The object that provides sexual satisfaction is not part of the instinct itself. The instinct drives the individual to seek out an object—the infant, for example, finds this object in his or her mother or other caregiver. At the mother's breast, the infant has an experience in which both the instinct for nourishment and the sexual instinct are satisfied. The manner in which a baby experiences this satisfaction is, for Freud, the prototype of every future love experience. The infant is fed, held by the mother close to her breast, caressed, kissed, and gently rocked; all this *tenderness* plays an important role alongside the awakening of *sensuality* that results from the actual physical care the infant is given—from sucking at the breast to stimulation of the genitals when the child is being bathed.

The two currents of sexuality: sensuality and tenderness

In a paper he wrote in 1912, "On the universal tendency to debasement in the sphere of love (Contributions to the Psychology of Love II)" (Freud, 1912d), Freud distinguishes two currents in sexuality: the *tender* and the *sensual*. Although this distinction appears in other writings of Freud, he explores the question in greater depth in his 1912 paper. The reference to tenderness runs through all Freud's writings, from 1888 until 1938—although the French- or English-speaking reader could hardly be blamed for not noticing the fact. The German word *zärtlich* has been variously translated, as have its derived and composite versions: the accurate translation—tender—has been replaced by approximations such as (in French) *affectueux, sentimental, adoré, amoureux* ... and (in English) by affectionate, loved, greatly loved, warmly loved, fond, devoted ... The word *zärtlich* and its linguistic variations occur some 418 times in the German edition (*Gesammelte Werke*) of Freud's writings, while the word *tender* and its linguistic variations are found on only 140 occasions in the *Standard Edition*.[4] In other words, the frequency of use in English is only one-third of that in the original German; this goes to show that insufficiently accurate translations can in fact obscure what an author actually wrote.

The second of Freud's "contributions to the psychology of love" discusses a form of impotence in men that manifests itself only with certain women and not at all with others. Freud shows that this outcome is caused by the failure to combine the two currents of sexuality, tenderness and sensuality. The tender current is the older of the two; it springs from the tenderness the child feels for his or her parents and other caregivers, and from their tenderness towards the child. This tenderness is not without eroticism, although in childhood eroticism is diverted from its sexual aim. "Then, at the age of puberty, the tender current is joined by the powerful sensual current which no longer mistakes its aims" (Freud, 1912d, p. 180). When the sensual current comes up against the barrier against incest (the parents, the child's first love objects, are prohibited as possible objects for sexual relations), it turns towards objects other than the infantile ones; tenderness and sexuality are then reunited. If a man remains fixated to incestuous objects, he will feel only tenderness and not desire for other figures who remind him of these prohibited objects. Sensuality is expressed only with respect to objects that are *debased*. In other words, such a man will be potent with prostitutes and impotent with women he respects and values, as he respected and valued his mother and sisters. *Mutatis mutandis*, the same argument applies to cases of female frigidity; Joseph Kessel's novel *Belle de Jour* (later made into a film by Luis Buñuel) is an illustration of this kind of frigidity linked to the dissociation between tenderness and sensuality.

Clinical practice confirms Freud's thesis; certain patients correspond in the minutest detail to the description Freud gives in this short but very important paper. Also, when we observe the relationship between infant and mother, we can witness directly sensual and erotic behaviour—and, when maternal tenderness is lacking, this aspect becomes excessive both in intensity and in frequency. All infants need a considerable dose of tenderness, and if they do not receive it, they tend to seek out excessively erotic means of gratification: intense and frequent public masturbation, various forms of auto-eroticism, erotic behaviour aimed at the mother (for example, rubbing the body in an almost ecstatic or orgasmic way against the mother's hair). Some very young infants can develop fetishistic trends.

This tender current is close to what some authors, following John Bowlby (1969–1980), have called *attachment*. Moreover, the adjective or adverb *zärtlich* (tender, tenderly) is often found, in Freud's writings, in close proximity to words denoting attachment, linking (*Bindung*) or dependence (*Abhängigkeit*). Although, for Freud, attachment is linked to tenderness, at the same time he insisted on the fact that every attachment is *ambivalent*: Thanatos is always mingled with Eros, hostility with tenderness, and hate with love. Those who uphold attachment theory have never come to terms with the fact that the balance between these two tendencies is always a delicate one, one which always has to be conquered afresh.

Narcissus

From about 1910, Freud began to acknowledge that the libido was not aimed solely at some external object or other, but also towards the ego, towards oneself: in everyday language, we speak of self-love, of self-esteem, and of egoism. In his paper "On Narcissism: an Introduction" (1914c), Freud begins with homosexuality (homosexuals need their sexual partner to be cast in their own image), then goes on to discuss certain difficulties encountered in psychoanalytic work with neurotics (who maintain their erotic relationship with their objects, but in fantasy), then schizophrenia (schizophrenics seem to have withdrawn their libido from people and things in the external world), and focuses on the idea of a "primary and normal [form of] narcissism". This leads him to the concepts of ego-libido—libidinal cathexis of oneself from the very beginnings of life—and object-libido, which is directed towards another. It should be made clear that, in the psychoanalytic sense of the word, an *object* is both an external person and part of internal reality—a combination of internal pattern and external person, a kind of synapsis.

The term *narcissism* is a reference to the myth of Narcissus, "a handsome young man who scorned love" (Grimal, 1951). Although some psychoanalysts contrast drives with narcissism, Freud considered that, alongside libidinal cathexis of the object, there existed a libidinal cathexis of the ego—in other words, that self-love and love for the other person both exist.

If the libido is directed exclusively towards the ego, death may ensue. "Narcissus came upon a spring and bent down to slake his thirst. The reflection of his face in the clear water was so beautiful that he immediately fell in love with it. Henceforth indifferent to the outside world, he bent down towards his reflection and allowed himself to die." (Grimal, op. cit.).

Narcissism remained a topic for reflection, as it were, long after Freud. Primary narcissism is not present simply because the baby is born; there is, of course, a vital force in the new-born that drives him or her to want to live, to seek out the breast, to ward off pain. Yet, if the baby is not looked after properly, that vital force may well be blocked or even reduced to nothing. Babies can cathect themselves libidinally only if they have experiences of well-being, the kind of experience that those who look after them—and above all their parents—provide. A baby who is not loved is unable to love him- or herself, to experience the feeling of on-going being as a whole person, and, later, to have self-esteem. This kind of self-love is not purely egoist in nature, it is the condition that makes possible feelings of love for other people. *In order to love, one must have been loved.*

Eros

Some ten years later, after the end of the First World War, Freud's thinking turned to life and death, to war, and to the traumatic neuroses that resulted from the war. Once again, his clinical practice and sensitivity towards what his patients were telling him were to generate new concepts that sought to explain the phenomena he observed.

Until then, human beings had appeared to Freud to operate according to two principles: the pleasure/unpleasure principle on the one hand, with its aim of avoiding pain, and the reality principle (adapting to external reality) on the other. But he could see that some patients repeated the painful experiences they had undergone; instead of trying to avoid them at all costs, they kept reverting to them in an attempt to gain mastery over them. This led Freud to think of mental life as a combat between two sets of opposing forces: on the one hand, binding forces that unify, create links and establish even greater unities, and, on the other, forces that strive to defuse or undo connections, to separate and to destroy. Freud gave these two sets of forces mythical names, *Eros* and *Thanatos*, because he considered them to be life-forces and death-forces respectively.

"Eros is the god of love [. . .]. Eros will always be [. . .] a fundamental force in the world. [Eros] guarantees not only the continuity of the species but also the internal cohesion of the cosmos itself. [. . .] Yet, far from being an omnipotent god, Eros is constantly dissatisfied and ill at ease." (Grimal, op.cit.). That is how Eros is described in Greek mythology.

Thanatos is death. Not all psychoanalysts subscribe to the idea of a death instinct. Life could de defined, according to Bichat (1800; 1994, p. 57), as "the set of functions that resist death"; its sole aim would appear to be to last as long as possible and to perpetuate itself. Although, obviously enough, death comes at the end of life, to argue that it is the *purpose* of life implies a radical change of emphasis. In his "metabiological" musings, Freud went on to define Thanatos as an instinct that tends towards preservation of an initial inanimate state, with the return of all living things to inorganic matter. "[I]nanimate things existed before living ones" (Freud, 1920g, p. 38).

Eros and Thanatos are locked in combat; ambivalence is the rule, not the exception. In this final version of his theory, Freud leaves us with two poles for cathexis and two modalities in which cathexis may operate: all instinctual forces are either turned inwards towards the self, or directed outwards (the ego and the object are the two poles); and cathexis may either be positive and libidinal (Eros) or negative and destructive (Thanatos)—the two possible modalities. Freud did not re-examine his earlier conception of narcissism in the light of these new ideas. If we do take a new look at the concept, it could be seen in terms of a happy and healthy kind of narcissism (libidinal cathexis of the ego), and of a deadly and pathological one (destructive cathexis of the ego). Pathological states of mind such as depression and the psychoses involve an incapacity for self-esteem and for self-love. The narcissistic defences of the grandiose ego reveal a failure to establish positive narcissistic cathexes.

From infantile to perverse sexuality

When Freud claimed that all children have a sex life, quite a storm broke out. What! These pure and innocent beings are involved in impurity and depravity! Yet it was not Freud who discovered the existence of infantile sexuality. The *Diary* kept by Héroard, the King's Physician, on the childhood of Louis XIII is a good example. What Freud did was to highlight the role infantile sexuality played in personality development and in mental health or illness. More generally, he argued that our childhood leaves traces that influence our adult life: the concept of *infantilism* is an important one, and is one of the cornerstones of psychoanalytic theory. The relationship one has with one's first two love-objects—one's parents—sets up an internal pattern to which external objects will later have to correspond: as Freud argued (1905d, p. 222), finding a love-object is to some extent a refinding of it.

Freud shocked his contemporaries. Yet, far from "driving people to crime" and encouraging unbridled copulation and promiscuity, he made only slow progress towards what now would be called a much more liberal attitude towards moral standards. For example, in 1909, instead of considering masturbation to be legitimate, he wrote that little Hans's mother, in repressing her son's masturbation, "had a predestined part to play" (Freud, 1909b, p. 28). Yet today, we invoke Freud's name when we say that masturbation is part of the normal life of children and as such should not be condemned. It becomes a cause for concern only if a child masturbates in a compulsive and public manner . . . or if parents are over-inquisitive as regards their child's masturbation.

For Freud, infantile sexuality possesses several distinctive characteristics. It is auto-erotic, it involves erogenous zones other than the genitals, and it attaches itself to one of the vital somatic functions. The infant sucking the mother's breast has erotic access to the breast which, at the same time, provides nourishment; the erotic breast is lost when the child is weaned. In 1905, Freud still thought that erotic satisfaction could be provided only through the infant's own body and not through contact with that of someone else. A little later, however, he acknowledged that the anal phase, when control over the sphincters is acquired, implies some relationship with a love object. The advent of genitality marks the primacy both of the genital zone over the other erogenous zones, oral and anal, and of object relations. What begins to take shape as the Oedipus complex blossoms, when the little four- or five-year-old boy announces to his mother that he will marry her, is reactivated at puberty, when full sexual relations—including impregnation—become possible.

The part played by the erogenous zones other than the genitals (in themselves sources of arousal and pleasure) does not disappear with the advent of adulthood. Kisses and caresses prepare the way for sexual intercourse, in what Freud called preliminary pleasures. The same is true of other component instincts—where gratification is linked to seeing or being seen, to suffering or making the other person suffer (masochism and sadism). However, if sexual pleasure is focused principally on these infantile modes of gratification, if it requires that the activities linked to these erogenous zones and component instincts always be practised, and if the only objective is the self's personal pleasure—instead of culminating in shared genital satisfaction in which the partner's pleasure is taken into account—Freud considered this to be *sexual perversion*. Nonetheless, he was bold enough not to dismiss sexual perversion as bestial, immoral and foreign to everything human—he attempted to explain it developmentally in terms of fixation at, or regression to, some aspect of infantile sexuality. Things that run counter to the barriers that our upbringing has erected (a sense of modesty, feelings of repulsion, condemnation) were not ipso facto censured by Freud, who regarded them as part of erotic life as long as they did not become the sine qua non condition for obtaining an orgasm.

Infantile sexuality and perverse sexuality are dissociated from the biological finality of procreation. Although Freud treated them as an integral part of human sexuality, he found it difficult to dismiss procreation entirely as the ultimate aim of sexuality [Freud 1916–1917 (1915–1917)]. In the 1890s, he had spoken of "actual neuroses" (neurasthenia, anxiety neuroses, hypochondriasis), linking them to disturbances in the patient's present sexuality (coitus interruptus, masturbation, abstinence, etc.). Patients who suffered from what he called transference neuropsychoses (hysteria, phobia, obsessional neurosis) told him about their childhood and spontaneously linked their adult problems to their childhood experiences. Neurotics are characterized by the fact that they prohibit themselves from doing something that perverts allow themselves to do: "Neuroses are, so to say, the negative of perversions" (Freud, 1905d, p. 165). This is where we enter into the complex world of human sexuality, which is always a *psycho-sexuality* in which fantasies and prohibitions are in constant interplay.

In human beings, no instinct, whether it be hunger or love, leads directly to satisfaction. This is not a characteristic feature of sexual life per se. Human beings eat (or refuse to eat) certain foodstuffs in accordance with the cultural traditions of the social group to which they belong—they may indeed die as a result of having infringed some taboo or other—and with their personal tastes, ideas and fantasies. In the realm of sexuality, their helplessness may go as far as not knowing how to make love, give birth and feed their children; their actions always refer back to models—either they follow the same pattern or they take it upon themselves, in fear and trepidation, to infringe them. In human beings, the world of representations, with their extensive range and variety, is incommensurate with the capacities of any animal. As Maurice Godelier put it, human beings function by representation.

Certain fantasies are called "primal" because they are shared by all human beings and refer to our origins: intra-uterine life, the primal scene (fantasized, not necessarily observed, sexual intercourse between the parents), castration, seduction. Children's inquisitiveness with respect to sexuality lies, for Freud, at the heart of intellectual curiosity. Consequently, it ought not to be discouraged; their questions should be answered honestly.

Depending on the circumstances, fantasies may open the way to sexual activity or erect barriers against it. That is why psychoanalysis is not a matter of applying technical recipes to sexual problems; its aim is rather to create the conditions that will allow the analysand's fantasy life to unfold and be explored.

Prohibitions may be neurotic—but they may also have a constructive dimension as far as the psyche is concerned. Neurotics prohibit themselves from carrying out acts that nothing in their cultural tradition or in external reality forbids. Others may transgress constructive prohibitions, such as those that require the difference between the sexes and between generations to be respected.

Sexuality, love and sublimation

If we go one step further than Freud, we could be tempted to equate Eros with love, but in fact this is only one of the aspects or ingredients of love. The erotic search for a partner implies that tenderness should accompany sensuality. Love is not reducible to sensuality, nor can it eliminate sensuality altogether. A subtle balance has to be found between sensuality and tenderness, between self-love and love of the object, between love and hate. In contemporary theory, we tend to think in terms of *Eros*, in which sensuality in its strictly sexual dimension plays the main role, of *Philia*, in which friendship and reciprocal tenderness are at the forefront, and of *Agapè*, in which love is selfless, with no sensual or egoistic aim, as in the love of God and of one's neighbour.

At no time did Freud argue in favour of unbridled, limitless copulation as the sovereign remedy for all our ills. "Copulation, revolution!" cried the characters in *Marat-Sade*, in a theatre production by Peter Brook shortly after the events of May 1968 in Paris. Lifting of social repression is not the same thing as lifting of its neurotic counterpart. Freud acknowledged the considerable role played by *sublimation*, in which sexual energy is channelled towards non-sexual aims. People may quite justifiably derive considerable satisfaction from their cultural, artistic and intellectual activities as well as from their efforts to help others. Freud went as far as to say that the ascetic anchorite "does not even necessarily display any pathogenic allocation of the libido" (1914c, p. 80).

The question remains open as to the extent to which it is possible to do without direct sexual satisfaction. Freud partly answered this question in quoting the fable of the horse of Schilda. The inhabitants of Schilda, heroes of a populist 16th Century German novel, had the reputation of being pretentious and somewhat simple-minded. In the fifth of the lectures he gave to an audience in Clark University, Worcester, Ma. in 1909, Freud (1910a, (1909), p. 54–55), explained that it is impossible to sublimate everything, and, to illustrate his thesis, he told the story of the horse of Schilda. The citizens of Schilda possessed a horse of which they were extremely proud, but which was very expensive to feed. They decided to reduce its ration of oats every day. The day they suppressed the final stalk of its ration, the horse died—and the citizens of Schilda could not make out what it had died of. In other words, complete sublimation is impossible: the sex drive, like hunger, demands at least *some* degree of direct gratification.

A limitation in Freud's thinking

Yet there is one limitation in Freud's thinking. Focusing on sexuality and sexual relations, he ignored the concept of and the problematic issues raised by *gender identity*. In his view, human beings belong so fundamentally to both sexes simultaneously that he felt the idea of "man" or "woman" to be completely abstract. The idea of *gender* as distinct from sex was developed in the 1950s. The division of the human species into two biological sexes (though there are some intersexed variants in the process), leads to a division in social roles. Some, like Françoise Héritier (1996, p. 19) go even further: "The observation that the sexes are different is the basis for all thinking, whether traditional or scientific". There is always an "I" who accompanies our thinking, and this "I" is not neuter; at any given point in time each of us feels him- or herself to be either a man or a woman—while we spend only a limited time having sex, however expert at making love we may be. Should we therefore conclude that "sexuality is everything"? No. But we cannot deny that it is a constantly active force, co-extensive with life itself. And on condition that we take both gender and sexuality into account, how could one not agree that sex makes the world go round ...?

Notes

1   Though his untimely death prevented him from completing his *Histoire de la Sexualité* (*A History of Sexuality*), Michel Foucault (1976,1984) casts doubt on the idea that, during the past three centuries, sex was subject to repression, both *per se* and as a matter for debate.
2   References to Sigmund Freud follow the *Standard Edition*, Freud Bibliography, notation.

3 The German verb *treiben*, from which the noun *Trieb* is derived, means "to be pushed" and, when used transitively, "to push". The Latin verb *instigere* or *instiguere*, from which derives the word instinct, means "to goad, to incite, to instigate".

4 The *Standard Edition* was published between 1953 and 1964, with an Index appearing ten years later, in 1974.

CHAPTER THREE

Gender identity

E very society draws a distinction between men and women, and sometimes also between other, minority, categories. Each of us has the intimate feeling of being either a man or a woman; some feel themselves to be in an ambiguous situation. That feeling was for long known as one's "sexual identity", but nowadays that term is more often used to refer to one's erotic inclination—homosexual, heterosexual or bisexual. Then the idea of "gender" appeared, followed by that of "gender identity".

The advent of gender

In grammar, of course, the concept of gender is by no means recent. Masculine, feminine and neuter dictate the rules of grammatical agreement between different parts of speech.

Gender is not a universal grammatical category (Corbett, 1991). To assume that it is is an ethnocentric illusion held by Indo-Europeans, all of whose languages have two or three genders. There are, however, many languages—notably Chinese—which do not have that notion; this does not prevent those who speak a genderless language from drawing a distinction between men and women. Linguistic gender does not create sex.

Gender in the sense of one's psychological or social sex appeared for the first time in John Money's 1955 paper, where he writes of "gender role": "The term gender role is used to signify all those things that a person says or does to disclose himself or herself as having the status of boy or man, girl or woman, respectively. It includes, but is not restricted to, sexuality in the sense of eroticism." (Money, 1955, pp. 254) According to Money (1985), it was Evelyn Hooker who, in an exchange of letters with him, first used the term "gender identity". Then—still according to Money—Robert Stoller advocated the "partitioning" between sex, which is biological, and gender, which is psychological and social, before going on to publish his two-volume *Sex and Gender* (Stoller, 1968, 1975). Stoller coined the term "core gender identity" to denote the feeling of being either male or female, which is established around 2½ years of age; "gender identity", the feeling of being masculine or feminine—more or less masculine or feminine—can be modified throughout one's life.

Money, a psychologist, was fortunate enough to work in the world's first paediatric endocrinology unit, set up by Lawson Wilkins in the Johns Hopkins Hospital in Baltimore. All intersexed patients from North America and beyond came to consult in that unit. The expertise that Money and his colleagues thereby acquired was quite outstanding. It was his study of the intersexed that led Money to introduce the idea of gender. Gender—the feeling that one is a boy or a man, a girl or a woman—does not derive directly from one's chromosomal formula, gonads, hormone levels, internal genitalia, external genitalia . . . in short, it does not derive from any biological feature whatsoever. It is a construct, a belief; those biological elements may play a part, but the crucial factor is the sex in which the child is raised by his or her parents, as long as they do so with conviction.

The problem of the intersexed

In about 1.7% of all births the biological sexual characteristics of the new-born do not match up properly—they are heterogeneous as regards chromosomes, gonads, hormone levels, internal and external genitalia.

The traditional way of deciding to which sex an infant belonged was to look between the baby's thighs and say "It's a boy!" if one saw a penis and "It's a girl!" if one saw a vulva and labia.

Trouble begins when appearances are ambiguous. The penis may be or may seem to be hypospadiac—the opening of the urethral meatus is on the underside. The testicles may be impalpable in the scrotum; they may be ectopic, located inside the abdomen. There may be a complete absence of penis and vagina, or a micropenis.

In some cases, the sex appears to be female—yet the child is male with an XY chromosomal formula (complete androgen insensitivity syndrome). That diagnosis can be made at birth only if there are other known cases in the child's family; the karyotype will then be checked, and further investigations undertaken. Until quite recently, these means of investigation were unavailable; no discussion was therefore possible as regards the sex to which the infant should be assigned.

If there are inconsistencies between the various biological components of sex (external genitalia, internal genitalia, gonads, hormone levels, chromosomes), how is one to decide to which sex that infant should be assigned? As I have pointed out, the decision used to be based on the appearance of the external genitalia; then in the 19th and 20th centuries, scientists began investigating gonad histology, followed by the karyotype. This "true-sex policy" has since been superseded by an "optimal gender policy". The idea is to determine with which gender the infant would, on the balance of probability, be more comfortable. Since it is easier to construct a vagina than a penis, a boy born without a penis might well find himself brought up as a girl, even though all his other biological sexual components are male. It is even more difficult to decide the issue when a boy is born with a micropenis; in such cases an assessment is made of its potential for growth in response to androgen stimulation. Some people, however, disagree with the idea of bringing up a male child as a girl.

Surgical procedures undertaken as early as possible have been recommended in order to make the external genitalia look as much like those of the assigned sex as is feasible. This factor is important for the child concerned, for the parents and for his or her peers.

Money and his co-workers have published data leading to the conclusion that this solution is a satisfactory one. Children experience themselves as belonging to their assigned sex, even if it runs counter to their biological sex, as long as their parents bring them up with conviction as members of that assigned sex (100 cases out of 105: see Money *et al.* 1957).

The intersexed used to be thought of in teratological terms, as errors of nature or developmental mishaps. In personifying nature in this way, we lock ourselves into a teleological perspective: a living human being is compared to some presumed blueprint of Nature said to represent an ideal model.

There are no true hermaphrodites in the human species: no one human being can possess a full set of characteristic features of both sexes together with the capacity to procreate in both of them— whereas this is the case simultaneously in snails and successively in some species of fish and shrimps. The term hermaphrodite is sometimes used to describe human beings who possess both ovarian and testicular tissue, but in fact they are only pseudo-hermaphrodites.

In Ancient Greece, Hermaphrodites was a god. In India, there is the composite figure of Ardhanishvara (Shiva united with his wife), in which the right half is male and the left female. There was nonetheless in Ancient Greece a contradiction between the androgyne, defined as "a very high state of nature and of the divine", and the fact that "there were certainly many children who were exposed, drowned, or burnt because their sex was doubtful at birth or seemed to change at puberty" (Delcourt, 1958). In many places, in actual reality, the intersexed, pseudo-hermaphrodites, were experienced as frightening and often put to death (Brisson, 1997).

The intersexed are not monsters; they are human beings, variations within the human species. Like some other sub-groups, they experience distressing limitations in life such as sterility.

The challenge to Money's norms

A certain number of intersexed patients in the United States were dissatisfied with the results of the surgical procedures that had been employed to operate on their genitals as young children (their erotic capacity had diminished) and complained that their assigned sex had been decided upon without their opinion having been sought. In the 1990s, they set up support and assistance groups, one of the most important of which is the *Intersex Society of North America*. These associations demand the abolition of the treatment norms introduced by Money and adopted to a great extent throughout the world. Money had been criticized for some time, in particular by Milton Diamond (1965).

The story of John-Joan as told by John Colapinto (2000) fuelled the arguments of those who were dissatisfied and had considerable repercussions. John was born a boy and had a twin brother. When they were 8 months old, both boys were diagnosed as presenting a phimosis and circumcision was recommended. John was the first of the two to undergo the procedure—the electrocautery appliance slipped and amputated most of his penis. It was decided not to operate on his twin brother. When his opinion was sought, Money's advice was that the child should be raised as a girl; his account of the case claims that the child adjusted perfectly to his/her new identity as a girl—he/she was henceforth Joan. There are photographs that show the child dressed as a girl. In actual fact, however, the boy rejected being identified as a girl; as an adolescent, he was told the truth about what had occurred. In the intervening years his penis had been completely removed, as had his testicles. In spite of that, Joan decided to live as a man. For about ten years everything seemed to be going well—he married a woman who already had three children. However—and this occurred after Colapinto's book was published—John later separated from his wife and, in 2004, committed suicide. His brother had committed suicide two years before.

That case brought Money's ideas—and the way he put them into practice—into disrepute. Bradley et al. (1998) have, however, published a report on a similar case of a boy whose penis was amputated, this time with a positive outcome in "her" new feminine identity.

The issues here are complex. It is equally impossible nowadays to support Money's position, as it is to adopt the militant standpoint of the *Intersex Associations*. The militant point of view tells us something about those who are unhappy with what has been done to them, but does not give us any indication as to what proportion of the whole group they represent. Follow-up studies are necessary; patients who have had some kind of help in childhood and adolescence should if possible be re-contacted; children could be asked to participate in prospective studies. Indeed, some case-reports of this kind are beginning to find their way into print (Meyer-Bahlburg et al., 2004; Richter-Appelt, 2004).

Transsexualism

Some people do not evidence any biological signs of being intersexed, at least according to our present means of investigation, yet they feel that they belong to the opposite sex from their assigned one. A biological male may have no difficulty in acknowledging that he has a penis and the body of a man; he feels, however, that he has the mind and soul of a woman and wants his body to be brought into line with his feminine identity—he wants his "true body" to be "given back" to him. Similarly, a biological female may have no difficulty in acknowledging that she has breasts, a vagina and the body of a woman; she feels, however, that she has the mind and soul of a man and wants her body to be brought into line with her masculine identity—she wants her "true body" to be "given back" to her.

Such people are in a very painful situation; they are afraid that others may think that they are mad. They particularly dislike any mention of "psychological disorder" when describing their experience. The militants of these support groups demand that psychiatry be kept well away from transsexualism and that the very term be removed from all manuals that classify mental disorders—the DSM-IV, for example.

They argue that the problem is a purely physical one, an error of nature; endocrinologists with their hormones and surgeons with their scalpel are the only ones who can alleviate the distress in which they find themselves. The pathos of that argument lies in the fact that, with the best will in the world, physicians can transform only outward appearances and not what is actually inside the body. Such patients will never be like men-born-men or women-born-women. As some transsexuals have said to me, in these real-life circumstances, it would be a significant progress were we to find a way of "changing what people have in their minds".

They are wary of any psychotherapeutic approach because they see it as guilt-provoking. Any suggestion, however tentative, that their present state may in part have something to do with the interactions between them and their early environment makes them feel that they themselves are being blamed for something. Yet no-one should feel more responsible for interactions that took place in early childhood than for the body with which he or she was born. In fact, it is no easier to remedy that situation: we come up against a "psychological bedrock" which is just as intractable as its biological counterpart.

Such patients, then, are searching for proof that their condition is of biological origin, that they have an intersexed brain condition—

their brain is feminine but their body is that of a male, or vice versa. They scrutinize every piece of research that points in this direction, even though these studies do not, when all is said and done, provide them with the "evidence" they both hoped for and announced.

What is a masculine brain, or a feminine one for that matter? Statistically, the results of psychological tests show differences between "average" scores of men and women in some domains: men, for example, do better than women in visuo-spatial tests. But looked at as a group, the scores obtained by men and women overlap—some women have excellent results while some men perform poorly. And anyway, what possible relationship could there be between these aptitudes and the *feeling* that one is a man (or a woman)?

Some researchers have studied the nuclei at the base of the brain, the role of which is well known in animals as regards their "sexual behaviour" during coitus. There is, however, a crucial issue here: no animal model of gender identity exists. The animal concerned adopts the sexual positions appropriate or not to its sex—but there is nothing to indicate whether or not the animal experiences itself as belonging to that sex, in other words as a male or female rat for example. Further, no-one knows exactly what role these nuclei at the base of the brain play in human beings.

One of the studies most often quoted is that of Zhou et al. in Amsterdam (1995). It was only after several years that they were able to examine a total of six brains of deceased male-to-female transsexuals. They discovered that the central subdivision of the bed nucleus of the stria terminalis—a brain area which measures some $2 \, \text{mm}^3$ and is smaller in women than in men—was, in the brains of the transsexuals they examined, the same size as or slightly smaller than that of women. This study is still awaiting replication.

According to Zhou et al., the size difference in this brain area may be linked to hormonal influence *in utero*. Other similar studies, such as that of Goy et al.(1988) in the University of Wisconsin, are highly regarded. In Goy's study, female rhesus macaques were androgenized either early in the pregnancy (days 40 to 64) or late (days 115 to 139). All the females showed some male behaviour but none of them the complete set of male behaviour (more mother-mounting, more peer-mounting, more rough play with peers, preference for initiating play with male partners, less grooming of mothers). A high level of androgen impregnation *in utero* occurs in individuals who suffer from congenital adrenal hyperplasia.[1] Studies have demonstrated that the genitalia of girls who suffer from this condition are ambiguous—clitoral hypertrophy that gives the impression of a misshapen penis—and the girls themselves manifest tomboy behaviour; their feminine identity, however, is not called into question. There is as yet no evidence that androgen hormone impregnation has occurred *in utero* in the case of female-to-male transsexuals; in addition, nothing goes to show that, even if such impregnation does occur, the outcome will be male gender identity.

The enigma remains unsolved. There may well be biological factors that facilitate or even generate cross-gender identity. One thing is certain: there are always interactions between a child and his or her environment. We see this in young children who reject their assigned sex but whose attitude can change once they and their parents have treatment—the innermost feelings of parents with respect to gender and sexuality do have an influence on their children.

One interesting hypothesis is that a phenotypic factor (i.e. one unrelated to genetic make-up) may play a role. Often, very feminine little boys who reject their assigned sex were once very beautiful babies, so much so that other people were inclined to say: "Oh, what a pretty little girl you have there!"; tomboyish girls who reject their assigned sex were often little horrors, restless and unattractive or even ugly in early childhood (Zucker et al., 1993; Findell et al., 1996). The physical appearance of such children seems to have facilitated certain kinds of interaction with their environment.

Gender inflation

The feeling that one belongs to a specific sex/gender does not derive automatically from biological characteristics; it is constructed in accordance with one's life experiences, so that gender is very much a social creation. In their struggle for equality of rights, women can turn this to their advantage: everything one says about women is social in origin and therefore can be criticized and revised.

Some sociologists have gone as far as to say that gender precedes sex. Would societies really have invented gender if there had not already existed two sexes? That reality is an indisputable fact; though called into question by the 1.7% of the general population who are intersexed, it is not disproved by their existence, given the part played by the differences between the sexes in procreation, upon which the very survival of any social group depends. The notion that "gender precedes sex" can be understood from a sociological point of view in terms of the fact that anything said about sex derives from some social representation or other; that much is true. Today when we speak of the body and of sex, we take as our basis a contemporary conception of biology—the social representation in our time and in our culture.

The body, however, precedes its representation in a conception which, for want of a better word, I shall call "materialist". I use the term without reference to philosophical discussions concerning materialism, and in my own way: thinking cannot exist without a brain, the mind cannot exist without a living body. All our thinking is influenced by culture. Expressing one's refusal to be a boy by wearing a skirt does not derive from one's genes or biology; it is a cultural expression.

Having dissociated gender from sex, some people now attempt to challenge not only gender differences but also those between the sexes, the existence of the sexes as such and, in the final analysis, the existence of gender itself. We should all see ourselves as trans-gendered, we should never accept any systematic attribution of a gender—as and when we like, we ought to be able to be man, woman, or both. This is the age of the "queer"—but not in the sense of strange, odd or homosexual; the word implies the absence of sex or gender, or having multiple sexes or genders (Chasseguet-Smirgel, 2003, p. 23).

Sexual orientation and gender identity

As is clear from the extract quoted above, Money included sexual orientation in his definition of gender, gender role and gender identity. He never varied on that point. If a male chooses another male as his sexual partner, or a female another female, this is what Money called gender transposition or gender cross-coding, even if in all other respects he or she behaves as a man (in the first case) or as a woman (in the second). "Many people have asked me this question and argued over the answer, which is that one must have some criterion of what is gender cross-coded and what is not. It is very widely accepted in society and in comparative life sciences that the criterion of sexuo-erotically uncrossed gender coding is this: the prevalence of males and females as sexual partners is greater than the prevalence of males and males or females and females as sexual partners. This prevalence applies across species." (Money, 1988a p. 103).

Everyday experience tends to show that most male homosexuals do not question their masculine identity; similarly, most female homosexuals do not question their feminine identity. For heuristic reasons if for no other, it is important to distinguish between gender identity and sexual orientation; only then will it be possible to study any relationship that may exist between them.

The claim that sexual choice constitutes one's identity can be challenged. Choice is a matter of fantasies, of desires, of behaviour; it is only from a militant point of view that we could legitimately speak of a homosexual identity.

Money's definition is useful in that it sees homosexual choice as a variant form of minority sexuality. Homosexuals have to deal with a threefold issue: (i) the persecutions to which they have been subjected, (ii) the fact that they constitute a minority group, and (iii) the fact that their sexuality cannot be procreative—if they are to procreate they need the help of someone of the opposite sex, whatever form that collaboration may take.

Male or female

Could the existence of the intersexed lead to the abolition of the distinction between male and female? Some people imagine that sex lies along a sort of continuum, but the truth is simply that there are a certain number of variants. A suggestion often made is that we should henceforth speak of the "third sex" or even of "third sexes".

The importance of maintaining the dichotomy between the sexes is underscored by the fact that, being separate, the sexes have to unite in order to procreate (*sexuality*). Biologists have pointed out that instead of *procreation*, the term often used is *reproduction*, which is in fact a misnomer, since human beings are not reproduced in an identical manner from generation to generation: there is no schizogenesis (the simple division of unicellular bodies), no parthenogenesis, and no spontaneous cloning in human beings. In procreating, human beings produce new creatures, each of whom is different from all others. Innovation is accomplished through the death of certain individuals and sexual procreation; sex and death go hand in glove with each other. Human beings give themselves the illusion of immortality, but they survive through the birth of other, different, humans.

For the species to perpetuate itself, each sex needs the other. The existence of biological sexes is thus extremely important for every human group. It should be pointed out, too, that human beings do not perpetuate the species as such, they perpetuate a social group, with its systems of relationships and representations.

Every cultural group has its own representations of the distinction between males and females. Caught up in the developments in science and scientific techniques that our civilization has promoted, we attach particular importance to biological findings. These, however, are constantly being revised, and we know nothing of what will be discovered tomorrow (except, of course, in science-fiction novels). Scientific knowledge can never eliminate fantasy, fuelled as it is by what has been handed down from ancient myths and by what some people call superstition.

The differences between males and females are quite clear; they pertain essentially to the genitals, the sex act itself, and procreation. A man has genitals that are external, visible (he shows them off with not a little pride), sensitive to aggression, and delicate as regards capacity for erection. A woman has genitals that are hidden and internal, and she cannot see them directly. Erection is a characteristic feature of men; it is quite ridiculous to draw a parallel, as is sometimes done, between nipple or clitoral erection and that of the penis. Men penetrate, and in order to do so they must have an erection; failure to do so is a blow to their narcissism—*men have to show their mettle*. Women must be able to adopt a receptive position and let themselves be penetrated. Men engender, women give birth; up till now, only women, like all female mammals, can carry children and breast-feed them. It is no doubt possible to imagine stratagems that would allow men to carry children in their peritoneum and to have milk in their breasts. Such devices, complex and expensive as they are, could never become the usual manner in which human beings procreate. With regard to other mammals, women have certain specific features: penetrability does not depend on oestrus, one day they will be menopausal and cease to be fecund. Cultural tradition attaches prohibitions to penetration, even though, biologically, penetration is feasible at all times—for example, during menstruation or pregnancy or immediately after giving birth. Society is always trying to limit and to regulate sexuality, yet at the same time sexuality eludes all attempts at control. Every society thus has contradictory attitudes towards sexuality.

In their sexual development, men and women are different. In women, the various stages are clear enough: their first menstruation, the rhythm of their periods, defloration, pregnancy, childbirth, breast-feeding, menopause. The keynote sign in all of these stages is blood—it either flows or ceases to flow. Women are forever *waiting*: they wait for their periods, the recurrence of which is independent of their willpower; they wait (or waited) for a husband to appear; they wait for the birth of their children, and then have no control over the way they develop; they wait for the onset of lactation . . . Given their receptive position in coitus and the fact that they have to wait for all these major events in life, women are thought of as being *passive*. Yet they have to be actively receptive when having sex—women are not inert planks of wood with a hole in them. They have to be active while breast-feeding. The fact that Freud equated femininity with passivity has led some of his epigones to conclude that, since women are active during breast-feeding, they are at that point virile—the epitome of absurdity, in which a characteristic feature of women is treated as a sign of masculinity! On the other hand, men, whom Nature forces to show their mettle when they have sex, are said to be *active*. And they have to show their mettle in a social context. The steps in men's sexual development are not marked by such abrupt transitions as in women: the occurrence of wet dreams and ejaculations cannot be compared to a girl's first periods; there are no visible indications of loss of male virginity; making love may well lead to the birth of a child without that event having repercussions in the male body—childbirth puts women to the test (and puts their life in danger), not men; there is no comparison between the so-called "male menopause" and the menopause in women—men retain the capacity to procreate, even though their semen may be less rich in good quality spermatozoids. Throughout the ages, society has subjected men much more than women to rites of passage and to long and painful initiation ceremonies, thereby creating social transitions to compensate for the lack of biological caesurae.

Man or woman

In *The Second Sex*, Simone de Beauvoir (1949) wrote that "One is not born, but rather becomes, a woman", a claim which is particularly apposite here—on condition that we apply it to men also. We are born male or female (or intersexed), we *become* a man or a woman.

It is not as easy as one might think to give a satisfactory definition of a man or of a woman. It is tempting to say that a man is a male who wants to be masculine and who, in order to be acknowledged as such, conforms—at least to some extent—to the criteria of masculinity laid down by the society of which he is part; similarly, a woman is a female who wants to be feminine and who, in order to be acknowledged as such, conforms—at least to some extent—to the criteria of femininity laid down by the society of which she is part. If we make do with these definitions, we fail to take into account the intersexed and transsexuals. They have taught us that it is quite possible to identify completely with the criteria of masculinity without being a male, or with those of femininity without being a female. In the end, it could be argued that a man is someone who feels himself to be a man, who wants to be one and who openly declares that he is one; while a woman is someone who feels herself to be a woman, who wants to be one and who openly declares that she is one. This goes to show how the situation of the intersexed and of transsexuals, which lies at the very origin of the introduction of the notion of gender, leads to gender inflation and, *in fine*, to the disappearance of the idea itself. Gender cannot be completely dissociated from sex—and indeed neither Money not Stoller attempted to do that. The problem is a difficult one.

What is beyond doubt is the fact that the criteria of masculinity and femininity vary from one culture to another. They have to do with appearance, clothes, attitudes, behaviour, language, feelings we are supposed to experience, psychological features we are supposed to present, activities for which we are deemed suitable, and status in society (political, economic, legal, religious). To take two extreme cases: war is almost always waged by men; childbirth is biologically women's preserve, and all a man can do is to imitate this in the *couvade* ("sympathetic pregnancy"). For just about everything else, there is always one society that calls masculine what another regards as feminine. This was conclusively demonstrated by Margaret Mead in *Male and Female: A Study of the Sexes in a Changing World* (1948).

Masculine and feminine do not result from the (biological) nature of men and women; they are an *interpretation* of undeniable biological differences. Though these interpretations may be purely conventional (and to a great extent arbitrary), they are imposed on the members of a given culture, and the majority tend to abide by these stereotypes. Why? Because if we challenge them, we run the risk of being rejected and excluded.

What is even more crucial is the fact that there is a hierarchy of values between masculine and feminine; Françoise Héritier (1996) calls this the "differential valence of the sexes". "Feminine" is everywhere held to be inferior to "masculine".

Yet the fecundity of women is an invaluable asset for every social group. When soldiers are needed, the birth rate has to rise—contraception and abortion are therefore forbidden. Women's mothering ability (breast-feeding) is needed in societies where animal husbandry is unknown (because there are no animals to provide milk); if the mother is unavailable, a wet-nurse must be found, a woman who can provide milk. In contemporary society, we are largely unaware of this, now that feeding-bottles and manufactured milk products mean that anybody—including men—can feed an infant.

Women, biologically prepared for looking after new-born children, are programmed for long-term attachments—a prerequisite for the survival of the infant. This creates a difference in the sentimental make-up (the emotionality) of women—in their emotions as Braconnier (1996) puts it. Perhaps that is one of the reasons for the fact that women seem to value monogamy much more than men do.

It is true, of course, that women have less muscular strength than men. The *difference in muscular strength* greatly impressed Simone de Beauvoir, who mentions it several times in *The Second Sex*. But how can that difference in itself justify treating women as inferior in every domain? And, when it comes down to it, in certain societies, hard physical work is reserved for the womenfolk . . . In social groups in which war-making and hunting were typical pursuits, physical strength obviously had a role to play; if a young boy was to become a man, he had to show his mettle by killing a lion or by scalping some enemy or other. We have moved on a bit since then. Machines have replaced masculine strength, and the nature of work itself has changed. If masculinity is associated with the idea of violence, if the human penis, very soft and lacking in bone structure, is regarded unconsciously as equivalent to a weapon, the reason is that men have wanted to control women and have at times penetrated them by force—and that they continue to do so in certain circumstances, either in everyday life or in war situations.

The fact that, in the absence of any aggression, blood flows from a woman's vulva is felt nonetheless—and by both sexes—to be a *wound* that she has to bear. On the walls of prehistoric caves (Leroi-Gourhan, 1971), the male genitals are symbolized by an arrow, the female ones by a wound. In addition, this wound arouses anxiety, for the blood that flows from it is brownish in colour, dirty, powerful because of its link with the ability to bear children, and dangerous because it may possibly be used to cast an evil spell. We only have to remember that even today in our own culture a menstruating woman is said to make the mayonnaise go off, or to be in danger if ever she goes for a swim or comes into contact with anything cold! According to Emil Durkheim, (1897), the taboo concerning blood, and more specifically menstrual blood, plays a role in the prohibition against incest. For Lévi-Strauss, (1949), the incest prohibition is a way both of ensuring that more women are available and of generating kinship ties by marriage. Following on from this, Françoise Héritier gives renewed importance to *humours* in the second type of incest: "Instead of, as in incest of the first type, there being a direct relationship—heterosexual or homosexual—between blood relatives, the second type of incest is indirect: it is no longer a matter, for example, of a son sleeping with his mother, but of a daughter coming into intimate contact with her mother if, by chance, she sleeps with her father or her step-father, or if her mother sleeps with her son-in-law." (Héritier et al., 1994 p. 9).

The penis, *sub nomine phallus*, is transformed into a symbol of narcissistic completeness—as if human beings should be considered whole only on condition that they possess a penis. That men value their penis is understandable. It is visible, its erection is impressive, the size of the father's penis is felt by the son to be impressive even though it may not be quite as big as a horse's (and little Hans developed a phobia of horses). A man can manipulate his penis; as a boy, he can play at who can "pee" the farthest; and verify that, after masturbating, it is still there—whereas little girls do not know what goes on inside their body. But why should it be made the symbol of wholeness for both sexes? Why should a woman be thought of as a "castrated man"? When we meet a man who has voluntarily decided on castration—a male transsexual, for example— we realize just how different a woman is from a castrated man.

Nonetheless, a truly feminine form of castration does exist— when a woman is unable to accomplish to the full what her sex potentially allows her: to be loved by a man and to bear children. In some cultures, sterile women are rejected out of hand, and even in our own, some women undergo distressing manipulations in order to be able to have children. It is true also that in many societies (Mediterranean, Muslim, Indian, Chinese, etc.), bearing children is not in itself sufficient—at least one of them has to be a boy. After the era of mother-goddesses, there was a universal overvaluation of the *penis*, with its transformation into a *phallus*; it is plausible to argue that such an overvaluation arose from a defensive reaction by men— unable to bear children—in the face of the impressive power wielded by women. When we listen carefully to what children have to say, we observe that, at about age three or four, little boys cry when they discover that they will never be able to carry babies in their tummy, nor feed them at the breast. Their desire to be a woman is firmly repressed, however, and they become contemptuous of and disparaging towards girls.

For both sexes, the discovery that there exist other human beings, as human as oneself, who have a differently-shaped body is traumatic. To make this discovery bearable, we need the help and mutual support of our own peer-group, and we need to denigrate the other group. If this were not the case, it would be impossible to understand the spontaneous segregation of children into two gender groups that takes place as soon as they go to kindergarten or playschool, even though they are being brought up in a co-educational environment. In addition to the anatomical difference between the sexes, there are other variations: in motor and verbal expression, in styles of action and communication. Each group is a puzzle to the other. Intolerance of difference begins in childhood, and the havoc it wreaks in adult life is well known—whether it be the gas chambers or ethnic cleansing.

The construction of gender identity

It was long thought to be self-evident that every young boy felt himself to be a boy destined one day to become a man, and that every young girl felt herself to be a girl destined one day to become a woman. Gender identity seemed simply to be the awareness of the sex to which nature and society, in complete agreement one with the other, ascribed to the child. It was, however, acknowledged that some cases were ambiguous, when, at birth, there was some hesitation concerning the gender to be attributed to the new-born: given the fact that attribution was at that time made solely on the basis of the appearance of the infant's external genitalia—before the advent in the developed world of modern methods of investigation—mistakes could be made. This would become obvious at puberty, if the child's development did not follow the expected path.

It was thanks to the intersexed that, in the latter half of the 20th Century, it was realized that, before being based on knowledge, gender identity is a *belief* deriving from the gender assigned to the child and from the manner in which he or she is raised: signs that could be taken to be self-evident do not convince a boy who has no penis that he is not a boy, or a girl who suffers from congenital adrenal hyperplasia and who simply has an oversized clitoris that she is not a boy too, if they have been brought up as boys by their parents in a convincing, continuous and coherent manner. The new-born baby does not know that he or she is a boy or a girl; it is the parents, on the strength of what the midwife or doctor tells them, who know this and inform other people of the fact. There is no attempt here to mislead oneself or others, unlike the situation described in Tahar ben Jelloun's novels *L'Enfant de Sable* (1985) and *La Nuit Sacrée* (1987). An indeterminate or misleading configuration really can exist. We have since learned that biological identity has many components and that these may branch out in opposite directions: chromosomes, internal genital organs, hormone levels, external genital organs, and, later, secondary sexual characteristics. Is any one of these biological elements to be considered more crucial than the others? It is astonishing to observe that psychological forces can prevail over biological ones. Sometimes, however, biological sex is the stronger element. This was the case with Herculine Barbin, whose story is told by Michel Foucault (1978). Some intersexed individuals who at birth have been assigned a gender that, though corresponding to the appearance of their external genitals, is at variance with their chromosomal and gonadal sex, and who have been brought up in accordance with their assigned gender, have later asked to be re-assigned as members of the opposite sex. But in many cases such individuals refuse re-assignment, because they feel they belong to the gender in which they have been brought up; their reactions may be dramatic if they are forced to accept re-assignment.

It would seem, therefore, that the feeling of belonging to one sex or the other is a belief. Later development usually confirms that belief, and the attitudes of those in contact with the child tend to reinforce it. But we see clearly that it *is* a belief when an individual asserts his or her assigned gender whatever biology says and whatever the assignment society makes; this is the case with transsexuals, who demand that doctors, with the help of hormones and surgery, transform them into members of the opposite sex—the sex, they say, to which they are convinced they belong. Their whole life is guided by their determination to belong to that sex. They claim that the soul is more important than the body when it comes to defining identity; yet at the same time they want their body to be changed—an impossible transformation—in order to rectify what they consider to be an error of nature. Symbolic membership of the opposite sex is not enough—they want a concrete marker, a bodily one.

In the case of very young children who reject their assigned gender, when we are able to observe parent-child interactions, we discover that the parents' attitude towards masculinity and femininity, together with their own sexuality, has an influence on their infant—who grasps something of the parents' inner experience beyond their manifest behaviour and interprets the conscious and unconscious messages they communicate. In constructing their narcissism, such infants can accept themselves only as members of the opposite sex.

This severe disorder of gender identity does not appear to result from castration anxiety (in boys) or penis envy (in girls). Besides, there would seem to be less concern about girls who are in difficulty over their gender identity; it is true also that, in our society, tomboy behaviour in girls is tolerated to a much greater extent than effeminate behaviour in boys.

Before we ourselves integrate our gender identity, it is there in the minds of our parents and other people in our environment. Our parents have desires and fantasies concerning our gender, and our family circle reacts differently depending on the gender that has been assigned to us. It is by deciphering these messages that we learn to which sex we belong. Knowingly as well as unwittingly, parents *shape* our behaviour by encouraging certain reactions and condemning others; by the time the child learns that these reactions are called masculine or feminine, he or she will already have learned which of them are to be repressed and which developed. It is true that our body provides us with sensations, and that these are not identical in girls and in boys. But what we feel tells us nothing about the other person's sensations.

Questions begin to germinate when the anatomical difference between the sexes is discovered. Some children manifest their rejection of their assigned gender even before they discover that difference, before what Roiphe and Galenson (1981) call the early genital phase, which develops during the latter half of the second year of life.

Rejection of sex assignment

In spite of the "differential valence of the sexes" and the denigration of the feminine condition, more men ask to be changed into women than women into men, though there are some variations in this sex ratio: usually the proportion is three men for every woman. At the time of writing, however, the number of women who want a change of sex would seem to be on the increase.

In what many of these people say, their horror at belonging to their given sex seems to weigh more heavily than the attraction of belonging to the opposite sex. That said, what transsexuals have to say about masculinity and femininity is remarkably paltry. Their whole focus is reduced to something like: "I'm a man. To be a man simply means being what I am", or "I'm a woman. To be a woman simply means being what I am". It is almost impossible to get them to add anything else, to obtain a description of precise characteristics or a statement of their own opinions. Their image of the role in society of men and women corresponds exactly to social stereotypes—which may go to show that it is hardly possible to challenge social stereotypes when one's whole aim is to be accepted.

What they do reject begins very early on in life. The boy is fascinated by his mother's "things"—her jewellery, her shoes, for example. No sooner is he able to walk than he wants to walk in his mother's shoes. He is already able to show that "gender" means something to him: his mother belongs to the same category as girls. In nursery school, he steals the girls' clothes. Observing his behaviour, we find it difficult at times to decide what belongs to the realm of self-identity and what should rightly be ascribed to the sensual pleasure he feels—a sensual pleasure bordering on ecstasy that, in later life, will be called perverse: there he is, lovingly stroking a fabric that seems to turn him on . . .

In our society, children's toys have gender connotations: some are neuter (soft toys, balls, Lego blocks, tricycles, roller skates, etc.), some are masculine (trucks, drums, Meccano sets, rifles, cowboy outfits, forts, etc.), and some are feminine (dolls, prams, tea-sets, nurse's outfits, etc.) (Tap, 1985). Dolls—and in particular the famous Barbie dolls—are feminine toys. Some boys' toys are used by girls—cars, marbles, etc.—but very few girls' toys are coveted by boys.

Styles of play and modes of communication are not the same either. Verbal persuasion is typical of girls, whereas boys are more inclined to use intimidation and force. Boys like to fight, girls like playing at mummy-and-daddy. The two sexes spontaneously segregate into different play groups from nursery school onwards.

The child who rejects his or her assigned gender wants to play with children of the opposite sex, and to be one of them. A girl may later go as far as to use a false identity in order to be admitted as a member of a sports club for boys; a boy goes off on his own and lets himself be bullied and called a *sissy*.

Sometimes it is only at puberty that a rather lonesome and ill-at-ease child becomes aware of his or her transsexual desire. Puberty is the definitive marker of belonging to one's assigned sex, and as such is unbearable. There is no longer any hope that a miracle might happen and that on waking up one morning one will find oneself a member of the opposite sex. Boys are increasingly persecuted because of their feminine appearance. Girls cannot stand the fact that their breasts reveal them to be women; they begin persecuting themselves by tightly wrapping bandages around their breasts (a painful thing to do), by not going to the swimming-pool or the beach, and by not wearing summer clothes in hot weather. Both girls and boys may even under-perform in school and refuse to sit exams under their assigned gender.

Transsexuals find themselves in an extremely painful situation.

Acceptance of sex assignment

The transsexual's dramatic rejection of his or her assigned sex is in no way comparable to the ordinary vicissitudes that just about everyone has to deal with.

When a girl envies boys, we call this penis envy, even though what she might in fact be envying is the status that possessing a penis confers on boys rather than the anatomical organ itself. In both cases, she still wants to go on being what she is—a girl with all the typical features of girls, plus that something extra: what boys have. Similarly, if a boy cries when he discovers that he will never be able to carry babies in his tummy, he feels envious towards his mother—but he does not want to become a girl; he would like to be able to have babies and breast-feed them while still remaining what he is, a boy. Core gender identity is established in the course of the first three years of life and is not thereafter called into question.

Thus we see ourselves as a boy or as a girl, in other words as male or female, and we then negotiate with ourselves and with others as to what is, or is not, acceptable in the stereotypes that society tries to force on us. We all have a physical resemblance to our parents, though usually more to one than to the other, whatever our sex; similarly, we identify with our parents' characteristic features and ways of functioning. We could say that we have psychic bisexuality as regards our self-identity. Some people try to struggle against what in their own make-up reminds them of the opposite sex, while others have no difficulty with this.

In addition, we have psychic bisexuality as regards sexual orientation. We have had relationships of tenderness with both of our parents; over and beyond *tenderness*, we have felt the desire to obtain from each of them the *attention* and *love* they gave to each other. This gave rise inside us to *sensual* feelings that fuelled the Oedipus complex in both of its directions—towards the same-sex parent as well as towards the opposite-sex one. When children fantasize, they feel sensations in their body, though they are as yet unable to decipher exactly what these mean. Infantile sexuality is *sexual/pre-sexual*, destined to become meaningful only as a *deferred effect* (*nachträglich*); the meaning of what is experienced can be grasped only once sexuality in the fullest sense of the word becomes possible, i.e. from adolescence on.

Accepting our gender identity is not a straitjacket; it requires a constant interplay between the sexes, an imaginative flexibility thanks to which we can see ourselves as a member of the opposite sex (which is not the same thing as the vital need to *be* a member of the opposite sex), we can identify with the other person and accept the idea of being to some extent like that other person without feeling threatened as regards what we in fact are. In order to accept psychic bisexuality, our mind has to work at it; but without it, our sexuality may never develop fully. I shall return to this theme in my discussion of couples and of the gap between psychic homosexuality and acted-out homosexuality.

Notes

1 A congenital defect in one of the enzyme systems that play a part in synthesizing hydrocortisone causes abnormal development of the adrenal glands and overproduction of androgens.

CHAPTER FOUR

From difference to equality

The observable differences between the sexes, some of which are established by society, are all based on the *sexual difference*, i.e. on the difference between the genitals, bodily substances (blood, sperm, milk), the experience we have of our body, the psycho-sexual cycle, relative status in intercourse, and the role of each sex with respect to procreation. The sexual difference is in fact the only *qualitative* one—expressed as all or nothing with the exception of the intersexed, who are very few in number the remaining differences are *quantitative*—they are expressed in terms of more or less—and statistical. For example, men are, on average, taller than women, but some women are tall and some men are short—there is some overlap between the statistical distribution of height in men and in women. Even though a woman may be tall, she is no less a woman for that; and though a man may be short, he is no less a man for that. Deviation from the average may be diversely appreciated, but it does not alter one's identity. A woman may well be upset if she is "too" tall; yet she will not be admitted to the *corps de ballet* of the Paris Opera House if she is "not tall enough". A man may have "no problem" with the fact that he is relatively short—or it may be the tragedy of his life.

In the psychological field, there are only a few statistically significant quantitative differences. If we study in detail the research findings dealing with the question (Maccoby & Jacklin, 1974), we see that they converge, emphasizing the following four relatively well-established differences as to sex:

1. Girls' verbal ability is superior to that of boys.
2. Boys are superior to girls in visuo-spatial aptitude.
3. Boys are superior to girls in mathematical ability.
4. Boys are more aggressive than girls.

It should be noted that cultural tradition plays a role here, and that girls' mathematical ability is at present inferior to that of boys only as regards certain subjects; in others, girls score higher than boys (Baudelot & Establet, 1992).

In itself, the sexual difference does not imply that one of the sexes is superior or inferior to the other; it implies complementarity, and this complementarity cannot be dismissed (as regards coitus and procreation, for example). Society has over the centuries ascribed complementary roles to each sex; this is particularly obvious in societies that have no tradition of writing—the distribution of tasks is such that the group itself could not survive without the presence of both men and women. Yet the "differential valence of the sexes" is everywhere present: the sexes have never been valued or treated in the same manner—women have been denigrated and oppressed by men. The crucial question—and Héritier does not discuss this enigma—is to understand why, since time immemorial, women have allowed themselves to be treated in such a manner by men, why feminism is such a recent phenomenon, and why some modification to the feminine condition has now become possible.

We shall therefore have to re-examine all that the sexual difference implies in order to discover what lies at the heart of the claim that men are superior to women and why this claim has been accepted by women.

The experience of one's own body

Men and women do not experience their bodies in the same way, and this is the case from their earliest years on. Their genitals provide them with very different sensations.

The principal features of the penis are that it is external, visible and erectile, and it can be manipulated. While the male foetus is still in its mother's womb, it has erections; babies, too, spontaneously or while being washed. A boy's penis is part of his body, yet it is not controlled by him. Very early on, boys have to face up to the fact that having or not having an erection is beyond their control; erections can occur even when they are not expecting one at all (Dumas, 1990, p. 13). The questions a boy may ask himself about the role of his penis are based on perceptual and sensual data. A penis that becomes "stiff" may well give rise to a schema of penetration—but what is to be penetrated, and how? The only orifices he knows anything about are mouth and anus. The experience of detumescence coming after an erection is enough to fuel his castration anxiety, even though no direct threats have been made (these are still sometimes uttered). When he sees a girl's genitals, he wonders: "Will it grow bigger?" Can it be that some human beings do not possess a penis? His mother, for example, such a powerful person, perhaps she doesn't have one? Boys, not girls, are the ones who devise the idea that there exists only one kind of sex organ, the penis.

Boys wonder, too, about the role played by their testicles; Dumas (1990) emphasizes how important it is that a boy's *father* explain to him the role that these "family jewels" (a slang term for the testicles) play in procreation.

A young girl's experience is in no way comparable to that of her male counterpart. Nothing is directly on display, and there is nothing to exhibit. She lives in the belief that she has something inside her body, if this has indeed been explained to her, and in the hope that one day she will be able to bear children in her womb and to breast-feed them. If she conducts a manual exploration, she will find a slit and a small, sensitive button; she will not find even two holes. Admittedly, as Kreisler (personal communication) has claimed, foreign bodies have been extracted from the vagina of little girls as young as two years, but this does not occur frequently. The sensations that the young girl feels are vague and do not enable her to "delineate" a vagina inside her. When psychoanalysts speak of *the unconscious awareness of the vagina*, we should not think of this as being rational, like a plate illustration in a treatise on anatomy. Nowadays, children are given true answers to their questions much more frequently than used to be the case; young girls have been shown what their body looks like inside. But it is only when she has sexual intercourse that a girl will really feel her vagina. Even menstruation does not give her a clear idea of what her vagina is all about. And when she is penetrated, she will never be able to reconcile that experience with what she saw in the treatise on anatomy, for the experience of being penetrated almost imperceptibly mingles vaginal sensations with anal ones. Lou Andreas-Salomé (1916) put it very aptly: the vagina is "taken on lease" from the anus. This combination of sensations is felt to be disturbing by some women and prevents them from having orgasms. Before this experience, in childhood, concrete representations of penetration can be constructed only with reference to mouth and anus; the navel is something of a puzzle and is sometimes thought of as the *locus* of penetration. Children may also imagine that the woman's tummy has to be opened (as a vagina that has been infibulated must be opened).

At puberty, the body changes, and the turmoil that these changes bring about in both sexes is well known. Once again, girls and boys do not experience things in the same way.

Both sexes see their body changing, leaving behind the kind of androgynous quality it had during childhood and asserting itself as male or female. Axillary and pubic hair grow, but only young men will grow beards—and that will come in due course. Their voices change: in boys, it breaks. The girl's breasts develop; if she has no gender identity disorder, she is delighted with this even though at times she may find it hard to cope with teasing remarks . . .

In boys, nocturnal emissions occur in just as involuntary a manner as do erections. Their first ejaculations in the course of masturbation are quite an event. It is important to remember that the same canal has both urine and semen running through it. When one of my patients, during a school medical check-up, was asked to urinate into a tube, he was filled with terror and shame when, instead of urinating, he ejaculated; his only way of extricating himself from that situation was to ask a classmate to give him half of *his* tube of urine . . .

Girls have their first periods, for which the English language has a word, *menarche*, which has no equivalent in French. "Losing" blood is no trivial matter. All the same, the dramatic descriptions of menstruation in Helene Deutsch's *Psychology of Women* (repeated by Simone de Beauvoir in *The Second Sex*) seem to me to reflect a time in our culture that now belongs firmly to the past. Most girls "wait" expectantly and impatiently for their first periods—proof that they are grown-up, that they are women—and are proud of them. The pain attached to menstruation varies greatly from one woman to another, and the inconvenience of having "periods" is not too difficult to manage. It is, nevertheless, a very particular kind of destiny. It is not difficult to understand the fact that the female genitals used to be represented by a wound, and that the experience of being a "wounded woman" could easily lead to acceptance of women's inferior status. This may well be more important than the fact of not possessing a penis.

The experience of sexual intercourse

The increase in sexual arousal is not triggered by identical stimuli —men and—women, nor are the conditions under which satisfaction is obtained the same. In Stoller's words, men are governed by "the urgency of stiff cocks" (1985, p. 35); men get a "hard-on" in response to visual stimuli such as striptease, where they can imagine the shape of the woman's body before it is actually unveiled to them when she takes off her clothes. Smells may perhaps play a part, but this is in no way comparable to the importance they have for animals. Women require some expression of tenderness; preliminary pleasures are particularly important for them, for the climax of satisfaction is not immediately reached. Men can be ecstatic when they "have it off" but not women. Men can have climactic pleasure in rapid-turnover brothels, an experience that is not open to women. A dialogue about sex is therefore not particularly easy to establish between two differently-structured types of sensitivity and sensuality. If there is to be a true meeting of minds, the strictly sexual dialogue will have to be part of a wider communication in which the partners not only talk about what they are feeling but also attempt to understand each other and adapt to each other's experience.

A woman, then, may easily have the feeling of being "possessed", sexually assaulted or even raped. In a case like this, the difference in physical strength between men and women may make her feel inferior. This physical inferiority, together with her lesser capacity for experiencing sexual ecstasy easily, may place her in a situation where the mind-set that is generated can make her think of herself as fundamentally inferior.

If men have to *show their mettle*—have an erection and one that lasts—women just have to *let it happen*. But sometimes that is not as easy as it sounds, because some women suffer from vaginismus, which blocks penetration. And just "letting it happen" is hardly likely to lead to pleasure. Of course, a woman can always resort to "lying"—only she can tell her male partner what it was really like for her, even though he may glean some hints here and there. Being "frigid" is not a fiasco comparable to not having an erection.

Pleasure comes from the whole atmosphere of tenderness, of the quality of the preliminary caresses, and of the man's expertise. Every woman has her own notion of what feels pleasurable. She wants to have an orgasm—but she will not always succeed, or perhaps she will not realize that what she is experiencing is in fact an orgasm. Sometimes a woman thinks that a true orgasm implies that she has to faint (leading experts in the field have said so), and since she didn't faint . . . Or perhaps she has heard that vaginal orgasm does not exist, so that she is convinced that she has never had one—even though what she is in fact describing is undoubtedly a vaginal orgasm. Or again, she may feel guilty as regards masturbation if, for example, she has masturbated by manually stimulating her clitoris; she needs her partner to caress her clitoris, but his caresses remind her too much of masturbation, so she cannot allow herself to have climactic pleasure (it is strange, all the same, that the same term—mastur-bation—is ordinarily employed both for self-caressing and for caresses given by one's partner). Her masturbation may, however, have been of a different kind, for example by using her thigh muscles without her hand coming into play at all. Freud had made this observation early on in his writings but then forgot about it when he equated the clitoris with an abortive penis, and feminine masturbation with masculine masturbation. In this case, the partner's caresses will not bring to mind her earlier masturbatory movements; a whole new sphere of sexuality is thus opened up in her relationship with her partner. Or again, even though she experiences a wonderful feeling of well-being, she may be ill at ease and dissatisfied: her sexuality does not resemble the extraordinary thing she had had fantasies about when she was a girl, intercourse between giants experiencing a gigantic pleasure, the giants of the primal scene—her parents imagined as two giants mating.

There are also fantasies that may or may not accompany sexual intercourse, as well as guilt feelings connected with the content of these fantasies. One of the components of these childhood fantasies is masochistic: in the scenario represented in the masturbatory fantasy, the young girl is often humiliated, beaten, and abused, and the climax of pleasure comes at a particular moment, variable according to each girl's scenario. Freud gave an example of this kind of fantasy in his paper "A child is being beaten" (1919e). That paper is often quoted as being the canonical form that every spanking or thrashing fantasy can take. However, this kind of fantasy may well take other forms, so that aspects other than those discussed by Freud are emphasized.

In that famous article, Freud alludes to the young boy's fantasy (he quotes two cases) but focuses more on those of young girls (six cases); we now know that he had analysed his daughter Anna (which, to contemporary analysts, seems astonishing; it can lead only to restrictions on the analytical process), who is in fact one of the girls quoted in the paper. According to Freud, the fantasy has three phases:

1. A child is being beaten; another child, a hated brother, is being beaten by the father.
2. The daughter is being beaten by her father (this phase, the unconscious origin of the fantasy, is reconstructed during the analysis).
3. Many children, usually in the girl's fantasy many boys, are being beaten by some anonymous figure, a father substitute.

For Freud, this fantasy has to do with the Oedipus complex and Oedipal guilt feelings.

It should be emphasized that it is usually the girl's back (though sometimes her buttocks) that is beaten; this refers of course to the corporal punishment she may well have had inflicted on her; to the helplessness that children feel during childhood—as well as to anal eroticism. In order to reach climactic pleasure, something has to happen to the girl, something she imagines that she does not control (even though, in the fantasy, she is the stage director and controls everything), something that awakens her anal eroticism, something that changes all the humiliations of childhood—in everyday life as in the Oedipal situation—into a triumph of some sort. Stoller deserves credit for drawing our attention to this latter component, firstly with respect to perversion (the desire to harm someone in order to ensure that humiliation will be transformed into triumph), and secondly with respect to sexual arousal in general, in which hostile feelings are often mingled with the erotic aspect.

In sexual intercourse, the woman waits for something that her partner will give her, a crucial difference with respect to the solitude of masturbation. Either she does not wish to be sexually assaulted, even though her masturbatory fantasies may have been masochistic; or she is to some extent willing to be assaulted because of the impact her fantasies have on her. The woman's position as regards sexual intercourse easily opens onto "masochism" which, when it occurs in men, is described as "feminine".

Woman and mother

Women can be mothers, men cannot. Freud did not perhaps ignore the envy that men may feel with respect to mothers, but he did underestimate it and almost certainly misunderstood its importance. Yet it is really quite common to hear a three- or four-year-old boy ask his mother: "Will I too be able to have babies in my tummy and give them milk?". In the face of her negative answer, he cries or at least shows that he feels upset. Women's capacity to be a mother is an object of envy for little boys, usually repressed and counter-cathected in adulthood; in the presence of a pregnant woman, a man has mixed feelings. A man may of course be happy to be a father-to-be; but he may also feel disgust at this body that gets plumper and plumper and more and more out of shape. He may be jealous of this rival for his wife's affections. The envy is present in rituals such as those of the *couvade* (sympathetic pregnancy), in which men are allowed to share the experience of pregnancy and childbirth. On one occasion I angered my audience very much when I said that pregnancy and childbirth mean that women have a bodily experience that no father can ever have, an experience that, even when it is a pleasant one, entails pain as well as danger (not so very long ago, dying in childbirth was quite an ordinary event); some young men in the audience protested that pregnancy and childbirth represented a dangerous experience for them too—the rituals of certain Indian tribes, they argued, were destined to protect men from the *symbolic* dangers entailed by pregnancy and childbirth.

In spite of all the scientific learning that is nowadays more or less common knowledge, pregnancy is still experienced as something of a mystery. We cannot control everything that takes place inside the womb; it fills us with both wonder and concern, and there is nothing we can do about it. In order to become a father, man depends on woman; and to be sure that the child really is his, he depends on what the mother says to him. A womb never ceases to be a disquieting antrum.

It is not difficult to understand the importance attached to the fecundity of women in ancient times. Faced with the cult of fertility and of mother-goddesses, it is understandable that men determined to assert their power: but not only did they emphasize the value of their penis, they went as far as to exaggerate its value as a Phallus. They claimed that it was men who played the more important role and that women were simply receptacles for their seed. Yet a man's body too is mysterious, for it is never entirely under his control.

In the book edited by Mathieu (1985), various authors show that in certain civilizations women have been forced to become pregnant over and over again in a dreadful state of subservience. The book points out that the only way a woman could free herself from this state was to be homosexual, thereby avoiding motherhood. However, motherhood is not simply a distressing experience that men force upon women, it is also a positive experience that women desire. Heterosexual desire exists too, notwithstanding rape and rape fantasies.

Every young girl knows that, like her mother, she will be able to have babies. More often than not she identifies positively with her mother, even though they may quarrel from time to time. A little girl likes playing with dolls. She can dream of the baby she will one day have, and although she may not realize it, the baby she imagines looks like her father—the child of her Oedipal dreams. Even though she is as yet unable to have babies and big breasts full of milk, she has been told that one day "it will all come to pass". Inside her, she has a hidden power, one that is invisible and turned towards the future. When boys show off their penis and play at who can pee the farthest, she has nothing to show, she has to *wait* and hope. The desire to have a child is a natural one, it does not have to be created artificially. Only adverse circumstances can prevent it coming to fruition or, as the authors of *The Hijacking of Women* claim (Mathieu, 1985), turn it into a mere consequence of an obligation imposed by men.

Women are biologically prepared to take care of infants. They secrete milk and, in civilizations where animal husbandry was unknown, the mother's milk (or that of some other woman) was vital for the baby's survival. According to Margaret Mead, some women, even when not themselves actually mothering, are able to stimulate lactation by putting an infant to their breast. Some women do not have enough milk to feed their baby or, for different reasons, prefer not to breast-feed. A mother's own milk is nonetheless best for her baby's well-being. The pleasure of breast-feeding, even though it tires a mother out, is felt to be a privilege by many women; it may even be felt as a truly sexual pleasure, something that tends at times to frighten those women who experience it as such.

The biological preparedness to take care of an infant is akin to what Winnicott (1956) called "primary maternal preoccupation": a mother feels her baby to be still a part of herself. Winnicott speaks of the positive value of this illusion for the child, who can experience the breast as being part of his or her own body: when the breast appears right on time in response to the pangs of hunger, the infant has the illusion of actually having created it. One day, of course, babies have to leave that illusion behind; and mothers have to be able to contribute to this necessary disillusionment so that the infant can go on developing.

A man may have motherly capacities, as long as he puts behind him the idea that babies are dangerous and could take away his manliness. But no man can be a mother.

Does this mean that a woman who has never been a mother is unfulfilled? When Evans-Pritchard (1965) was asked to write an apologia for a famous feminist, he found himself in a quandary: he wondered what, in winning the right to participate in the same activities as men, women in our culture have in fact lost—they have willingly remained unmarried and childless, whereas, in primitive societies, all women married and bore children. Evans-Pritchard forgot the tragic fate of sterile women or, in certain societies, of women who did not give birth to boys. Freud argued that no woman overcomes her castration complex until she has borne a son; although this is debatable, it is true to say that there are societies in which a woman is given consideration only in so far as she is the mother of a male child (sometimes too, a man has to father a son in order to finalize the various stages of his developmental cycle: henceforth an adult male, he can play a full role in society).

In our own culture, there are women who, whatever the constraints imposed on them by society, feel that they could not live if they did not have children. They want to be mothers, whatever the price to pay, and have recourse—far beyond what would be reasonable—to various techniques of medically-assisted procreation. Some important people have approved the fact that a woman of 60 wants to become a mother. The techniques we have at our disposal become much less effective with women over 38; but the physician lets him- or herself be tempted by the exploit; the woman wants a child, and on what possible basis, the argument runs, could we be justified in refusing—individual desire is its sole justification. Yet in this particular desire for a child, the narcissistic component (wanting a child for oneself) is much more important than the object-related one (wanting a child for him- or herself): the woman wants a child for herself and pays little heed to the fate she is creating for the infant concerned—elderly parents who are very likely to die before the child reaches adulthood, and even if they do survive (given the present increase in life expectancy), because of their age they will weigh heavily on their child's future instead of being a source of support.

No woman should be regarded as incomplete because she would appear to be a castrated man, or because she is not a mother. More than having the experience of something lacking, she above all has to experience the feelings her body offers her, feelings that are different from those of a man. Motherhood was always reckoned to be potentially on the horizon of every young girl's life long before, for reasons to do with choice or through some impossibility or other, it started to become obvious that she would never in fact be a mother.

What does it take for a woman to feel that she really is a woman, to feel fulfilled *qua* her sex? Conditions of this kind may be personal to the woman concerned or be imposed by the society in which she lives. In some cultures, sexual or other mutilation has been imposed on women; the pressures have been so strong that women not only submitted to this mutilation but also demanded that it be carried out in order not to be excluded from the life of the community. I am thinking for example of the practice of binding women's feet in ancient China, a practice that has now disappeared; with their toes folded under the soles of their feet, women were crippled, unable to walk normally (and to run away, perhaps?)—but no man would have married a woman with "big feet". Reducing the size of the foot is symbolically equivalent to sexual mutilation (Freud was right to see the foot as a phallic symbol). I am thinking also of more openly sexual kinds of mutilation (clitoral excision, infibulation of the labia); anthropologists have taught us to respect the originality of cultures that differ from our own, but it is difficult to remain impassive when faced with this kind of mutilation that sometimes puts a young girl's very life at stake. Whatever help we may be able to offer them, the interested parties themselves must take the initiative in fighting against such practices—and indeed some African women do just that; but there are many who remain convinced that mutilation of this kind is beneficial, that it does not diminish the pleasure they feel, and that it makes giving birth easier . . .. When, after migrating, Africans try to hold onto these practices, they find themselves caught up in a culture conflict, and fail to understand why the French penal system condemns them. Willing to accept the benefits of French law when it comes to social welfare, they do not feel obliged to respect that same law when it runs counter to their traditions; their cultural adaptation is both incomplete and conflictual. This goes to show the strength of cultural representations of what a woman should be. In societies where clitoral excision is practised, the idea is to remove this male part from women; following Freud, the clitoris is equated with a little penis. Having an abortive penis is not sufficient castration for women, the little bit they do possess has to be removed too, such is the fear that women inspire, such is the need to control them and to control when they are to bear children (a woman must not masturbate, she must not feel pleasure, there must be no risk of her going with any man other than her master and owner, her husband, and therefore of giving birth to children that are not of his seed). Behind the claim that women are inferior lurk such fear and envy of women's power that they have to be made more inferior still, mutilated and brought under control.

In our culture, in which sexuality quite openly plays an important role and a woman's right to sexual pleasure is accepted, it is difficult to imagine that a woman can live a full life without sexual intercourse. I shall ignore the insulting jokes heard in medical units when a woman, no longer young but still a virgin, consults a doctor; those so-called jokes bring nothing but shame upon those who make them.

After centuries in which people were made to feel guilty about sex, we now have another conception of it—but one which makes it difficult for us to understand that some people may willingly renounce all sexual activity (and here the problem is not fundamentally different for men and for women). Is it one of the criteria of mental health that sex should be part of life, and that our sexuality be a happy one? Freud drew the conclusion that sexuality was always one of the factors in the psychic conflict experienced by the patients, male and female, who consulted him; but he wrote too, as I mentioned in chapter 2, *supra*, that abstinence "does not [. . .] necessarily display any pathogenic allocation of the libido" (Freud, 1905d). Obviously, a woman who has never had sexual intercourse, like one who has never given birth to children, has not had certain experiences that undeniably form part of the sexual difference. However, nobody can ever accomplish *all* the potentialities of his or her sex; *a fortiori*, with the exception of Tiresias and other mythical figures, all the potentialities of *both* sexes.

Man and father

A man cannot be a mother, but he may be a father. For men, fatherhood often counts enormously, but it is not a physical and bodily experience comparable to motherhood. What does form a core part of a man's physical experience is the nature and quality of his early relationship with his mother, his intimate contact with the body of a woman. Some have argued (Stoller, 1968; Greenson, 1968), that, with such close proximity to his mother, the young boy has initially a feminine identity, one from which he has to free himself in order to become masculine. Freud thought of mothers as essentially seducing their children, including of course their sons, because they arouse sexual sensations in the course of bathing them.

It is quite true that, traditionally, many societies consider that over a more or less lengthy period of time all children belong to the universe of the womenfolk; then there comes a moment when the male child has to be removed from this world of women, from the *gynaeceum*, and be stopped from clinging to his mother's apron strings, in order to make a man of him through associating with other boys of his age and with men of various ages. A girl does not have this break in her relationship with her mother; Freud thought that the only way she could change her love object—turn away from her mother and towards her father—was for her to blame her mother for not giving her a penis. According to Stoller, this change in the love object, which has seemed to some to be a difficulty in the young girl's psycho-sexual development, is less of a problem than the change of identity that boys have to deal with, given their primary feminine identity. To subscribe to this theory requires a very particular conception of identity: the infant sitting on the mother's lap would seem to be impregnated by femininity, as a result of intimate contact with the maternal body. If this intimacy has been particularly intense—a skin-to-skin experience of blissful symbiosis—the boy may not be able to free himself from his feminine identity, so that he could claim to be a girl (and, later, a woman) without feeling it an insane thing to say, because it would be entirely in keeping with his initial identity; for Stoller, this is the kind of pattern that leads to true transsexualism. I believe, however, that we can have—that we ought to have—another idea of identity. Identity is a *construction* that children build up by integrating what they experience in their body with what their parents (and others in the environment) communicate to them either through direct behaviour or via faint and often unconscious messages that bear witness to what they (the parents) feel deep down inside. The boy who does not acknowledge his identity as a boy is not so much a boy to whom one or other (or both) of his parents has said that they would have preferred him to have been a girl, as a boy who has been advised in a very subtle manner not to behave like a boy and not to manifest anything that, in our society, has masculine or virile connotations. This is how *shaping* (Stoller) takes place. The sex of their as yet unborn child is present in the parents' minds before birth takes place, and the infant has bodily sensations; but nothing defines what he or she feels as specifically masculine or feminine, nothing that will help the infant to realize that there are two ways in which one's body is experienced and to put a name on that experience—nothing, that is, except what the parents (and, by extension, others in the child's environment) feel and what they say about it.

We have known for a long time now that there is more motor discharge in baby boys than in baby girls; we know too, that they are accepted much more eagerly than are similar manifestations in girls: "It's a boy, look how strong and aggressive he is already!" The attitude of those in the immediate circle is by no means neutral, it is sexually structured in accordance with the expectations of society as regards boys on the one hand and girls on the other. Although the greater muscular strength of men is a physiological rather than a psychological characteristic, women are by no means indifferent to it: either they praise it as in the example quoted above, or they emphasize it, as Simone de Beauvoir does in *The Second Sex*, or they see in it proof that men are potential brutes and rapists. Communication by violence and fist-fighting comes very soon to stand in sharp contrast to communication by verbal persuasion, and constitutes one of the reasons why children divide spontaneously into two segregated groups when they attend co-educational schools: from nursery school on, without any adult ruling on the question, children separate into gender playgroups in the playground; Maccoby (1990) sees in this a consequence of the fact that modes of communication are sex-specific. I would add that the discovery that there are two sexes—that human beings are both alike and yet dissimilar—is a traumatic one; in order to cope with it, children need to fall back on their same-sex peer group, proclaim the superiority of the group to which they belong, and denigrate the other group.

Baudelot and Establet (1992) show that the tendency to denigrate the opposite sex lasts all the way through to adolescence, at which point interest in and sexual attraction towards the opposite sex intervene. In adulthood, women still feel something that Claude Habib expresses very well in the opening pages of her book *Thoughts on Prostitution* (1994, p. 5): "I'm climbing the stairs in the Montparnasse railway station. A group of squaddies appears at the top. Some of the soldiers are unsteady on their feet; they are singing "Zero! Zero! Zero!" or else "Demob, for fuck's sake". One of them might throw a beer-can from the top of the stairs. I'm afraid of them. It's a group of men who have lost control. They could turn on me at any time, just like that, for no reason at all. Or maybe they'll just walk on by without even noticing me. My fear is unquestionably sexual, and I hate them because of this fear they are making me feel, a fear—I can feel it in my bones—that cannot but divert me from what I desire, push it down even more deeply, make it even more indecipherable, more withdrawn. As they pass by me, the hatred I feel for them is racist: I hate the smell of them, their masculine dirtiness, their body hair that is so different from mine, the loudness of their voices."

When he is still a very young child, the little boy is encouraged, pushed and in fact almost trained to assert himself. As I have said, in intercourse a man has to show his mettle: he has to have an erection—and one that lasts, one that enables him to penetrate his woman partner. Various civilizations have taken as their model that particular feature of sexuality and have constantly demanded that boys show their mettle. A boy has to be physically enterprising, take risks and never cry if he hurts himself. He will undergo initiation ceremonies that are sometimes cruel—but they will toughen him up; compulsory military service was an example and initiatory "ragging" in modern society is a caricature of that aspect of life. It may however be dying out, perhaps because we are beginning to forge a different idea of masculinity related to the decreasing importance of a man's physical strength both for consumer production and for military defence.

Men too desire to have children, and certain aspects of this are comparable to those of a woman's desire to have children. The baby is meant to *repair* the parents, to accomplish everything the parent has not succeeded in doing. Moreover, parents have the impression of surviving through their child, of being able to face up to death in a different way because they feel that, somehow, they are henceforth *immortal*. In societies where the father passes on his surname to his offspring, this transmission is important for men. Handing down one's fortune is also important for both parents (in the cognate line of descent prevalent in our culture, with respect to kinship, the ascendants of both parents are treated as being on an equal footing); the efforts they have made throughout their life become meaningful. Although not directly physical and bodily, the link between a man and his infant child is still extremely important; we are surprised to learn that a man's wife or cohabitee—the partner with whom he has spent most of his life—is often less important to him than his offspring, perhaps because a father feels responsible for their coming into the world (replacing one's partner always remains a possibility, but one cannot replace one's children, one does not divorce one's children), perhaps because of everything they represent—inter alia, proof of his virility (sterility is such a blow to men that for long the fact that sterility might be due to the male partner could just not be contemplated: sterility applied to women and only to women).

Nowadays, "modern" fathers take pleasure in looking after babies and, from birth on, are much more involved in bringing them up. The impact of this change in attitude has not yet been evaluated, especially in cases where circumstances are such that the father is in fact the "primary caregiver". A father is not simply a mother substitute, and parental roles cannot be looked upon as interchangeable. The specificity of the father's role as such is still very much present because, since man and woman are the two forms human beings can take, they make the child face up to the fact of belonging to one or other of the sexes: they force him or her to take on board the fact that there are two different ways of experiencing life.

The issue could be dealt with on a purely concrete level perhaps, given that not having a father is a well-known risk factor for children: in many cases of social deviance and pathology, fatherless children are in the majority. It is no more than a risk factor, and some children can overcome this handicap—the "resilience" of human beings, as we say today, is considerable, and children are able to overcome some extremely adverse circumstances. However, to take such a risk deliberately is unreasonable; it is quite enough not to be able to avoid it, as when the father disappears for one reason or another.

The issue could be looked upon from a symbolic perspective. Society makes the raw biological fact of sexed procreation meaningful and, in our civilization, acknowledges that children are the products of two lines of descent. Illegitimate children are no longer stigmatized for something for which they are not themselves responsible, and natural as well as legitimate descent are both recognized.

If a woman can be a woman without being a mother, *a fortiori* a man can be a man without being a father because, although fatherhood is part of ordinary experience, it does not involve the man's body as such in the way that motherhood involves the woman's body.

What I have said about sex pertains also to men. The sexual experience may be so important that one may put one's life in jeopardy in order to have such an experience. Jacques Lanzmann (1976) tells of how, as an adolescent, he was haunted by the idea that he must not die before making love to a woman. The story he tells is quite remarkable, both from the point of view of the author's style of writing and for the glimpses it gives us of adolescent psychology. He was in fact arrested in a police raid on Jews and driven off in a truck to what might have been his final destination: a death camp. What made him decide to jump out of the moving vehicle—with the risk of fatal injury—was this thought: "I do not want to die before I have made love to a woman". That in fact saved his life. (Though this is a story of a man, it could equally well have been that of a woman.).

Neither man nor woman can know what sexual intercourse is like without having experienced it. This does not mean that the first time one has sex reveals the whole potential of sexual relations—a continuous experience that depends on circumstances, feelings, choice of partner, settling down in life as a couple. Adolescents, middle-aged men and elderly men do not experience sex in the same way.

The change in women's status: facilitating factors and remaining obstacles

To believe that denying the existence of differences leads to the establishment of equality is to forget that differences are a question of *fact* whereas equality is a question of *rights*. Men and women are different sexually, yet this does not imply any clear difference in their characteristics and aptitudes. Everything, including differences in brain structure and functioning, is subject to quantitative variation; there is an overlap between males and females in the statistical distribution of these variations. Every society has felt the need to define gender roles, i.e. the masculine and feminine characteristics to which individual members must conform if they are not to be excluded from the *socius*. In fact, every society has defined what the sexual roles should be in the practice of intercourse. Culture is part of the very nature of mankind; development of one's potentialities requires the assistance of what cultural traditions have to offer (language, transmission of knowledge and of techniques). In human beings, a much greater part of their instincts is determined by environmental and cultural factors than is the case for animals, where, although the environment does play a part, there is no cultural heritage to hand down (instances of transmission in monkeys of some acquired abilities can hardly be compared to that, in human beings, of oral and written language, as well as scientific and technical knowledge). Societies have interpreted the sexual difference in terms of inferiority and established unequal rights for men and women.

Equality is not something that has to be proved, it has to be established, and this requires challenging the manner in which the differences between men and women have been interpreted, as well as calling into question the aberration of presuming to base rights on mere facts.

Were we to ask ourselves what has kept women in a position of such inferiority, there would be no end to our questions. It would be more profitable to consider what enabled this inferior status to be challenged in such a radical manner that it can no longer be seen as natural nor as dictated by divine right. There has been an out-and-out revolution, and even though it has not yet had a universal impact, there is no way the clock can be turned back.

With the *Declaration of the Rights of Man and of the Citizen* (26 August 1789), the French Revolution played a decisive part in this by challenging the established order of things and by calling into question the traditional divine right of the King. It is true that "man" had the meaning of *vir* (the male) rather than that of *homo* (human being), that the *Declaration of the Rights of Woman and the Female Citizen* by Olympe de Gouges (in September 1791) had no lasting impact, that, with the Napoleonic code (French civil code, 1804), women— eternal minors and legally *incapax*—were once again subject to male domination, and that, in France, women were given the right to vote only at the end of the Second World War. But a breach had been opened, and once civil if not civic rights had been obtained, a process was on the march; it did not progress spontaneously, however, but required the militancy of women, helped by some men, from Condorcet to John Stuart Mill.

A simple change of ideology would not have sufficed; changes in technology, however, have redefined the very nature of work. Over the past two centuries, industrialization has made actual physical strength less and less of a necessity in the manufacturing process. A computer workstation suffices for initiating and controlling production. This does not mean that manual work has completely disappeared, but many tasks that, formerly, could be carried out only by men, are now being handled by women.

The capacity of women to replace men in the workplace first became apparent during the First World War and marked a turning point.

Throughout the 19th Century, women were allowed increasing access to education. In France, a law of 1836 requested mayors to provide schools for girls, to be run by the local authority; since, however, this was more an invitation than an obligation, many preferred to leave that task to the Church, since the local authority would not, in that case, have to pay the staff. The requirement to provide primary school education for girls in every local authority area of more than 500 inhabitants was established by the Falloux law of 15 March, 1850, and firmly restated in the Duruy law of 10 April, 1867. The provision of secondary education was to come in several stages: 1863, 1879 (creation of 67 training colleges for women primary school teachers), and in particular via the Camille Sée law of 21 December, 1881 (high schools and colleges for women students), and 1883 (the prestigious training college at Sèvres for women teachers in higher education). But it was not until 1925 that girls and boys had the same curriculum (Arnaud-Duc, 1991, p 95). From then on, girls could sit the Baccalaureate exam and go to university. Prejudice, however, dies hard: after claiming that women's brains were inappropriate for learning Latin, at a time when Latin was the key to entering university, it was later said that women were impervious to mathematics, at a time when mathematics was becoming a top priority; I have already pointed out what lies behind this kind of argument.

The end of the Second World War saw the speed of technological transformation increase rapidly. The housewife's daily chores were lightened thanks to various appliances. In the old days, washing the laundry took up a whole day: going to the wash-house, letting the bundle of clothes "bubble" (boil) in a vast tub, scouring the laundry with a brush and rubbing it by hand, letting it "blue" in another tub, hanging it out in winter in a warm room and in summer in a drying shed—and, in this case, coming back the next day to bring it in (in the film *Gervaise*, we see a wash-house like that, the kind I knew when I was a child). Shopping for foodstuffs was done on a daily basis, because refrigerators were unheard of. I could go on and on making a list of everything that now makes everyday life so much easier. In former times, women were either slaves to domestic chores or "bourgeois", i.e. they could free up some time for themselves by handing over some of the tasks to another person. However, we should not delude ourselves: even in this day and age, in spite of all the appliances and in spite of the fact that men tend to share some of the domestic chores, daily life in most cases imposes a heavier burden on women than on men.

Science and technology have made progress too in the field of biology. Infant mortality has decreased and it is no longer necessary for women to spend their whole life going from pregnancy to pregnancy in order to have children who would survive (some women hardly ever had periods). In addition, methods of contraception have become incomparably simpler and more effective than the empirical means to which, from time immemorial, women have always had recourse. At least for the moment, these new contraceptive methods are the prerogative of women, who therefore plan and regulate their own pregnancies.

However, the fact that such methods exist does not mean that all women find them easy to use. Some women may feel upset—tradition and certain religious notions lay a burden of guilt on them, and they are unsure about how innocuous these methods of contraception really are. Diaphragms require a minimum of hygiene and comfort, but this is not the case for the pill—yet women have been made to worry about the possible consequences of the hormones involved. It would nonetheless be better to use contraception than to resort to "termination of pregnancy".

In France, the 1975 Veil law, which authorized termination of pregnancy, can be seen as part of the progress that has been made as regards women's position in society. Die-hards would not agree. Anyone who has had to help a mother who, feeling that she just could not cope with another child given the circumstances in which she lived, had endangered her life by putting herself in the hands of a "back-street abortionist" because she did not have the money to "abort" in proper conditions of hygiene and security, knows that making termination of pregnancy illegal is a form of social injustice. It is up to each individual woman to avoid the risk of having to seek an abortion if her conscience forbids it; but no one has the right to make this decision for her—and, above all, no man has the right to make this decision for a woman. In a certain number of dramatic circumstances (rape, incest), forcing a woman to keep the child is tantamount to being doubly violent towards her. Even when circumstances are not as dramatic as these, it is well known that men have often shifted responsibility for the consequences of their sexual actions, while this is just not possible for women (being a woman is not just a matter of her not having a penis, but also of having a uterus with all the consequences this may entail).

The fact that rights and responsibilities with respect to children now legally involve both parents (as distinct from the father alone) is also a turning point. Some people consider that we have gone a step too far in granting such rights to the child's mother when she and the father are not married. Indeed, some men have gone as far as to create associations for the "defence of the masculine and paternal condition".

It is clear, then, that in order to bring about a change in the status of women, several conditions had to be met: the struggle had to cease being that of isolated individuals, an unprecedented shift in ideology had to occur, the nature of work had to change, women had to have access to the same formal education as men, progress in biology and medicine had to reduce the rate of infant mortality thus enabling more children to survive and pregnancies to be planned, and these planned pregnancies had to be decided upon essentially by women themselves.

There remains one bridge that women still have to cross. They have quite specific guilt feelings about combining what, in society, has always been considered feminine on the one hand and masculine on the other: having children *and* a high-level professional career. Many women have always worked: farmers' wives, small shop-keepers' wives, working-class wives. But this is not the same thing as acceding to "prestigious" jobs and positions of responsibility. Even when there are no institutional obstacles, women curb their own ambition, independently of the bias that some people continue to have against them.

This brings us to the great question: what made maintaining women in an inferior status possible for so many centuries? What convinced women themselves that they were inferior, thereby contributing to keeping them in such a position?

Men's physical *strength* is greater than that of women. As for differences between the sexes, this is a statistical one reflecting averages: some women can have great physical strength—in Russian circus troupes, women can support a whole pyramid of men on their shoulders. But if individuals are to be selected in terms of their strength, women are not in a position to compete with men. This is well known in the field of sport. There have even been problems relating to sex change, either by returning an intersexed female to her original male biological sex, or because a male transsexual reassigned as a woman has attempted to participate in women's events: the intersexed ski champion, Schienegger, won a medal in a women's event, was some years later diagnosed as a biological male, and had to return the medal, which was attributed to the competitor next in line. There is also the case of René, who became Renée and, as a male competing against women, easily won several tennis tournaments.

Behind strength lurks *violence*, in other words *misuse of strength*. Not all women are trained in combat sports—it is easy for men to intimidate them. Nowadays people like to highlight—in films and in reality—women officers in important positions in the police hierarchy, who are called "the boss" (feminization of work-place titles has still to apply to some jobs).

In contrast to men's greater physical strength, women are less prone to psycho-biological weakness. There are fewer deaths *in utero* of female foetuses; fewer perinatal and infancy deaths of girls, fewer severe forms of childhood diseases and days spent in hospital; and women tend to live longer than men . . . Some have attempted to explain these facts in terms of an evolutionary model: females bear children and protect them.

However, pregnancy and breast-feeding mean that women— temporarily but repeatedly—need the protection of men, particularly in societies where life is harsher than in ours. Even in our society, women are well aware of the fact that, at such times, they like to have the support of their husband. Even though they may have desired a professional career and in fact are working, they are tempted to give it up in order to raise their children. Sometimes they do so, and with pleasure, but then they go through a difficult time when the children grow up and leave home—they would like to go back to their old job, but find themselves more or less unqualified because of the years during which they were not professionally active, and have difficulty in finding suitable employment. They become depressed. The best way of combating this depression is to help them find another job.[1]

As I have said, women are envied by men; their envy of women's capacity to bear children—of their fundamental power of creativity— is repressed. That is why women are felt to be dangerous; they have to be oppressed in order to repress the fear and the envy that they engender.

Yet even as men were crushing women under their superiority, they were recounting in their mythology tales of how women were originally superior to men. Godelier (1982; 1986, pp. 70–71) describes the message contained in the legends of the Baruya: "In the beginning, women were superior to men, but one of the men, violating the fundamental taboo against ever penetrating into the menstrual hut or touching objects soiled with menstrual blood, captured their power and brought it to the men, who now use it to turn little boys into men. But this power stolen from the women is the very one that their vagina contains, the one given to them by their menstrual blood." "All these myths thus confirm the pre-existence of a feminine creativity, in terms of time as well as in terms of those things invented which today give to men their superiority, for example, flutes, bows, salt. But these myths also stress how this creativity was capable of stirring up disorder. It could not benefit the community as a whole unless men stepped in; they did so, using violence, theft, and murder." (ibid., pp. 71–72).

One of the aspects of women's power and dangerousness has to do with blood. I have shown how her sexual life is constantly marked by blood: first periods, menstruations, defloration, giving birth—all these imply blood. When blood stops flowing, women sometimes attain the status of men. Blood, of course, is treated as a major taboo. According to Durkheim (1897, p. 50; 1963, p. 85), the prohibition of incest derives from women's blood and the taboo surrounding blood: "The blood is taboo in a general way, and it taboos all that comes into contact with it. [. . .] Thus the woman, in a rather chronic manner, is the theatre of these bloody demonstrations. The feelings that the blood evokes are carried within her; we know in fact with what extraordinary facility the nature of the taboo is diffused. [. . .] A more or less conscious anxiety, a certain religious fear, cannot fail to be present in all the relations which her companions can have with her, and that is why these relationships are reduced to a minimum." [. . .] [T]he woman, so to speak, passes a part of her life in blood." (op.cit., p. 53; 1963, p 90).

When a woman loses blood, she goes through a very special experience. As we have seen, her genitals may appear to her as though she has been wounded in that particular spot, and the wound may seem to be inflicted once more as she is deflowered—which itself has often been subjected to taboo. Menstrual blood is brownish in colour and dirty, and a woman who is having her periods is subjected to all kinds of prohibition. The residues of all this in our own culture go under the name of "superstitions": a menstruating woman makes the mayonnaise go off, she should avoid swimming, having any iced drinks, etc. In India, she is not allowed to enter a temple. Women, then, are treated as though they were carrying some sort of stain—and they let themselves be convinced so easily that this is in fact the case.

Bodily substances, says Godelier (1982; 1986, p. 232) "scream, and, from one point of view, sexuality is an indiscreet echo chamber for relations of oppression and exploitation". In the Baruya, the main task of menstrual blood is to provide irrefutable "proof" of the fact that women are victims of themselves—and of themselves alone. And women can only agree to that. "For indeed a Baruya woman has merely to see the blood start to flow between her thighs for her to hold her tongue and mutely consent to whatever economic, political and psychological oppression she may be subjected" (ibid., p. 233). One of the key words in that quotation is the notion of "consent".

I have the impression that feminists[2] are reluctant to admit that women have consented to their own oppression. They think that men are the obstacle, but the feminist revolution will be brought to completion only if women become aware of the obstacle that is inside themselves and take steps to overcome it.

One of the aspects of this internal obstacle has to do with the nature of female sexuality. It has often been said—by, inter alios, Freud himself—that female sexuality is passive by nature: libidinal trends with passive aims. In my view, the contrast between activity and passivity is inappropriate when it comes to describing sexual relations. A woman must actively agree to being receptive; she desires the experience that can only be offered her by someone else—but this requires also the help that she offers him: "Put me in," says her male partner. I have already mentioned the fact that, as regards childhood masturbatory fantasies involving being beaten, the masochistic component[3] is always ready to ally itself with female sexuality.

Towards equality

One revolution has been accomplished, although, in my opinion, its key issue was not so much the conquest of some possibility or other as the awareness that nothing could justify the fact that women were to be regarded as inferior beings. Women—but not all women—are now aware of that, as are some men. In his description of the Baruya, Godelier emphasizes just how important it was to become aware of this: "We all know that, when it comes to oppression, the domination of one section of society by another (sex, caste, class or race) is fully justified and legitimate only if the victims themselves become the guilty parties, those primarily responsible for their own fate." [Godelier, 1982 (1986, p. 232)]

The progress accomplished in Western society as a whole should not be played down, particularly as regards the freedom and rights that have been conquered—"woman's liberation" is the accepted term. I was very surprised to hear Simone de Beauvoir, just a few years before her death, talk as if nothing had changed.

True, not everything has changed—not for all the women who live in the western world as we know it, and even less so for women who belong to other cultural traditions. The ideology of revolution has enabled some degree of equality to be established. Yet, in China, little girls are being put to death—of course, they tell us that this happens only in remote country areas (it is true that, in Beijing and elsewhere, fathers are obviously delighted to walk about cradling their daughters in their arms). Yet, if a profession becomes typically feminine, people are underpaid and discredited—the prime example being the medical profession in Soviet Russia. Wage equality should be easy to set up—equal pay for equal work—but women are employed in positions that require much less training than they possess. Top-level jobs are rarely offered to women, but, aside from the question of maternity leave, women themselves contribute to this state of affairs by holding themselves back. The majority of medical students are women, yet there are only a few women who hold top-level positions. For example, there was only one women out of a total of thirty-two members in the section of the National Council of Faculties of Medicine at the time I belonged to it, and when all sections were taken together, there were only five or six women out of approximately 200 members in the whole Council. I mention these figures because I was myself surprised when I walked into the council room and saw so few women. In psychology, 80 percent of students are women, but this proportion is not maintained as far as university professors in that discipline are concerned (though here the figures are less distorted than in medicine).

The debate concerning parity is a topical one. Perhaps some compulsory measure is required in order to provide women with the opportunity of accepting positions of political responsibility that they are perfectly capable of taking on.

Another topical debate concerns the feminization of the names of trades and professions. For long, I felt reluctant about this demand, because I am not convinced that simply changing words is enough to change actual situations. Yet it is true that in Quebec, where people are fastidious about this kind of thing (in the university, the plate on the door of the professors' room carries both feminine and masculine forms of the word: *professeures* and *professeurs*), women are more active in politics. Marina Yaguello, a linguist who has written on the topic of words and women, was interviewed by Pascale Krémer for the *Le Monde* newspaper (7 July 1998). She said: "We need to name things in order to conceive of reality and to integrate it. I do not know if the feminization of words really does help women's advancement or facilitates women's access to positions that carry these new names. But I think it is symbolically important to accompany such advancement in this way." That is a reasonable way of putting it, in my view. With or without the approval of the *Académie Francaise*, we shall have to prepare ourselves to change our verbal habits, if by so doing we can contribute, however slightly, to women's struggle for equal rights.

Women's worst enemy is fundamentalism, whatever its nature. My conversations with Algerian women students taught me that their number one concern was the condition of women: their very survival depends on it. Women who live in countries where they are treated as inferior or even as slaves are much more numerous than we "liberated" women are—and we should never forget that, not even for a moment.

Essentialism or constructivism

The reader may think that I am adopting an essentialist standpoint because of what I see as a fundamentally important fact: that the sexual difference is inscribed in one's body and one's biological make-up. This is not the case; I am simply saying that no human being, man or woman, can exist other than in a living body. This is a materialist standpoint from an ontological point of view; it does not imply the primacy of biology as far as one's destiny *qua* man or woman is concerned. The reader may now think that I am adopting a constructivist approach, since, for me, everything that is called feminine or masculine is defined as such by the society in which men and women live, and only the fact of being male or female is decided by nature. Being a man or a woman is not simply a matter of being male or female. We are fortunate in that we live in a society that gives individuals much more freedom to decide on their own destiny. I think that human beings are defined by what they actually do with themselves on the basis of what Nature and Society have given them and with the understanding that these basic elements set up limits that cannot be ignored. I am therefore arguing in favour of a materialism that does not exclude ideals: what is most valuable does not belong to the domain of raw data. We are obliged to *postulate* the existence of freedom, otherwise human life would be meaningless and no possibility of changing oneself, by psychotherapy or through the experiences that life offers us, would ever exist. Nonetheless, I do not believe that freedom in this sense can be absolute—free will—although some philosophers argue that this is a necessary postulate (for example, Luc Ferry, in Comte-Sponville & Ferry, 1998). We have at our disposal only a little gradient of freedom, a *clinamen*, the little deviation in the fall of atoms described by Lucretius; we are faced with a series of micro-choices that, although apparently minor in scope, nonetheless give direction to our entire destiny.

Notes

1 Evelyne Sullerot has set up an association called "Back to Work", the aim of which is precisely that.
2 I do not mean that I am not a feminist. I am a feminist when it comes to fighting for equality of rights. I am not a feminist when it comes to advocating a *feminine-ness* that implies hatred of men and their ultimate banishment.
3 This component is exaggerated in the "erotic" book by Pauline Réage (Dominique Aury) (1954–1972).

CHAPTER FIVE

Choice of partner

"There is no instance of a society not regulating the practice of sexuality, within marriage and outside of it, as if it were important never to let things go too far," writes Luc de Heusch (in de Lannoy & Feyereisen, 1996, p. 251). Loss of *oestrus* in the human female, thereby uncoupling sexual desire from the reproductive process, could have opened up the way to sexual freedom or, in Godelier's words, generalized sexual intercourse.

This, however, is not the case; sexuality in human beings is restricted by social constraints as well as by internal psychological ones. There is no instance of a society that has not laid down rules concerning marriage unions, and more often than not those rules apply also to pre-marital and extra-marital relationships. In addition, the manner in which sexual intercourse takes place, the time, the place, the customs that apply to sexuality—these too are the stuff of beliefs, rituals and taboos that individuals are of course tempted to infringe, although sometimes this is no easy matter (death may result from infringing a taboo, even without the involvement of any external sanction). Furthermore, individuals create neurotic prohibitions for themselves.

The prohibition against incest

Something of man's generalized sexuality has to be sacrificed, says Godelier (Godelier & Hassoun, 1996, p. 10). "It is not the murder of the Father that I would use as a metaphor, but the notion of sacrificing something to do with "wild" sexuality; this sacrifice is what enables human beings to be co-responsible with nature for their existence as social beings, because they are co-producers with nature of the conditions of their existence. No animal species ever does that." "Man does not simply live in society, he produces society in order to live."

The prohibition against incest is a universal one, even though no universal definition of incest exists. For Lévi-Strauss, this is proof of the involvement of culture as distinct from nature. It has been pointed out that, in the case of great apes living in social groups, the mother ape will refuse to take any of her sons as sexual partners, as though imposing a kind of interdiction on herself. However, in these social groups, although the mother is known, the father is not. Thus this situation is in no way comparable to the complexity of kinship and of the prohibition against incest that we encounter in the human species; classificatory kinship relations do not exist in the animal kingdom. The prohibition against incest consists in forbidding marriage between certain relatives. This concerns certain classes of family member, not kinship defined in terms of true consanguinity. For example, cross cousins (children of the father's sisters or the mother's brothers) are treated differently from parallel cousins (children of the father's brothers or the mother's sisters)—the former may be preferred spouses, the latter forbidden. In our own culture, both sets of cousins are first cousins, and the degree of consanguinity is the same. This fact alone enables us to rule out the hypothesis according to which the prohibition against incest is the expression of an instinctive awareness of the noxiousness of marriage between blood relations; in fact, this noxious aspect occurs only infrequently, in cases of recessive hereditary defects generating the disease in homozygotes (who carry the same gene on each of the two chromosomes).

Durkheim had already challenged the idea that consanguinity played a role. According to him, exogamy (the obligation to marry outside the clan to which one belongs) results from a set of beliefs and rites that have to do with the blood taboo: "Thus, this gross superstition, which caused man to attribute to blood all sorts of supernatural characteristics, has had a considerable influence on the moral development of humanity." (Durkheim, 1897, p. 68; 1963, p. 112)

In *The Elementary Structures of Kinship*, Lévi-Strauss (1949) suggested that exogamy should be thought of as an exchange to ensure that every man, or almost every man (because polygamy means less women available), will be able to take a wife. It should be pointed out that, according to Lévi-Strauss, it is the menfolk who exchange the women, not the other way round. In a recent book, Maurice Godelier challenges the universal nature of the exchange of women between the menfolk and goes on to argue that kinship relationships are not in themselves sufficient to lay the foundations for social groups; religious and political relationships must necessarily play a part too (Godelier, 2004). For Lévi-Strauss, the prohibition against incest is simply the negative side of an exogamous rule that has positive consequences: it lays the foundation for the atom of kinship and the society of human beings by combining kinship by marriage and kinship by direct descent (this combination does not exist in the social groups of animals). By giving his sister to another man instead of marrying her himself, a man is sure of obtaining two sets of brothers-in-law—his sisters' husbands and his wife's brothers—who will be his companions at work and allies in times of war. Lévi-Strauss went on to explore the different systems of kinship in terms of variations due to transformations within a combinatorial arrangement the aim of which was to ensure the movement of women. The intricacy of what could be called the cognitive unconscious of human beings has to be admired; through the creation of different systems of kinship, it always ends up accomplishing the same objective.

Françoise Héritier (1994; 1999, p. 266) has studied another kind of incest—incest of the second type; the kind we have just discussed is called incest of the first type. However, the very existence of second-type incest has been seriously called into question by other anthropologists (Godelier, op. cit.). Second-type incest seems to Héritier to be crucial because "it is impossible to understand incest of the first type other than in terms of the second type of incest". "Incest of the second type affects, rather than unites, two blood relations or two relatives by marriage through the intermediary of a common sexual partner." This could be the case, for example, "of a man who sleeps with two sisters or a mother and daughter, to whom he is related neither by blood nor by marriage". From this perspective, "the fundamental incest, so fundamental that it can only be expressed approximately, in texts as well as in behaviour, is mother/daughter incest. The same substance, the same form, the same sex, the same flesh, the same destiny" (ibid., 1999, pp. 306–307). Here it is no longer a question of women being made to circulate, but of humours circulating, bodily substances, traces left by coitus. Oedipus committed incest of the first type by sleeping with his mother, and at the same time incest of the second type by ploughing in his mother's body the furrows that his father had ploughed before him; he was put in contact with his father's substance through his father's wife. Here we are in the presence of something I would tend to call an affect unconscious, which is closer to the kind of unconscious that we deal with in psychoanalysis.

The mother, then, "is the cornerstone of the prohibition against incest" (de Heusch, 1990, p. 244). For Godelier (1996, p. 52), the feminine dimension is doubly at the origin of the social beings we are. On the one hand, it is in women that the ontological transformation whereby sexuality was freed from *oestrus* took place; and on the other, every individual, man or woman, can fully become him- or herself only by separating from the maternal figure. For Godelier, the law cannot be identified with the Father. "In no society do all forms of power coalesce in one single figure, be it that of the Father or that of the Mother—and even less that of the fantasy substitute for men called the Phallus." [1996, p. 52]

Lovemaps

Each person's sexuality has its own idiosyncrasies, for which John Money coined the term "lovemaps". These include the particular characteristics of sexual arousal—what increases it, what makes it decrease afterwards—of choosing a partner, and of forming a couple.

In the past 20 years, John Money has created many neologisms, of which *lovemaps* is one of the best. He himself says he invented the term in 1980, and in 1986 he published a book with the title *Lovemaps. Clinical Concepts of Sexual/Erotic Health and Pathology, Paraphilia, and Gender Transposition in Childhood, Adolescence, and Maturity.* He says that, sooner or later, the word will be included in the dictionary because each one of us has a *lovemap* although we may be unable to define it. It is "an idealized and highly idiosyncratic image". The lovemap "depicts your idealized lover and what, as a pair, you do together in the idealized, romantic, erotic and sexualized relationship. A lovemap exists in mental imagery first, in dreams and fantasies, and then may be translated into action with a partner or partners." (ibid., p. xvi). "A lovemap is not present at birth. Like a native language, it differentiates within a few years thereafter." This implies that it is influenced by interactions with others; it can be vandalized by adults and, according to Money, it is particularly fragile between 5 and 8 years of age. This leads to hypophilia, hyperphilia and paraphilia—disorders of sexuality through inhibition, compulsive excess, or deviance (perversion).

Money is not a psychoanalyst, and he does not like the vocabulary of psychoanalysis (he does not like our talking about "object relations" because he feels that the word "object" lowers the status of the partner to that of a thing). However, with this conception in which the lovemap has its own history that depends on the interactions between significant people in the environment, Money is very close to psychoanalytic thinking. Much of what he has to say would remind us of Robert Stoller, although it is impossible to decide which of them influenced the other; more specifically, Money emphasizes a feature that is shared by all paraphiliac (perverse) lovemaps: the requirement that tragedy be changed into triumph (Money, op.cit., p. 36). This is also Stoller's main thesis in his *Perversion. The Erotic Form of Hatred* (1975).

Stoller has often spoken about scenarios—the plot that is played out in daydreams and in masturbatory fantasies. In his book *Sexual Excitement: Dynamics of Erotic Life* (1979), he explores and clarifies a masturbatory fantasy in a patient he calls Belle. It can indeed happen that an analysis focuses on the clarification of a masturbatory fantasy; the importance Moses and Eglé Laufer (1984) give to what they call the "central masturbation fantasy" in adolescence is well known.

Money speaks of images, Stoller of scenarios, i.e. of plots, but they are both referring to the same psychic reality. In addition, Stoller speaks of *scripts*, i.e. scenarios plus detailed descriptions of all necessary stage directions.

Psychoanalysis can succeed in elucidating—partly if not completely—the origins of detailed aspects of a lovemap, of the choice of partner, of the scenario, and of the script; by the same token, through the transference experience, it can succeed in modifying them.

In spite of its name, the lovemap is not concerned solely with the loving and tender part of sexuality but also with its sensual and erotic aspect. It includes precise details that increase arousal to a climax; these details are present in the individual's fantasy, and may be necessary for accomplishing the sex act (or, on the contrary, they may not be tolerated at all at that point). The relationship between fantasy and act is another difficult issue, in particular when perverse fantasies and perverse acts are involved.

In the choice of partner, the problem lies in the fact that lovemaps tend to fit in with each other. Thanks to what minute, subliminal signs do two partners feel the correspondence between their lovemaps? Sometimes they perceive the disharmony between them but disregard it, with ultimate failure of their relationship thrown in for good measure.

A fairly striking example of this ability to perceive something of one's partner's innermost nature, without any words having been exchanged, is given by Joyce McDougall in *The Many Faces of Eros* (1995). A patient, Marie-Madeleine, had refused all sexual intercourse until she met her husband; it so happened that the only erotic activity that interested her husband was "to have her urinate on him" while he masturbated her with his fingers. In the analysis, Marie-Madeleine recalled a childhood memory: "when she was between three and four years old, three playmates, all boys, persuaded her to take off her panties and climb up a tree so that they could look at her genitals", then they asked "please show us how you do a pee". She had been proud of her demonstration and of the excitement that it had aroused in them. But just at that point her nanny arrived on the scene, spanked her, and told her parents what had been going on, leaving Marie-Madeleine feeling deeply humiliated (op. cit., pp. 46–47).

Choice of partner's sex as an element of the lovemap

If we consider the lovemap to have a developmental history, we should also accept the fact that both heterosexuality and homosexuality have a developmental history. The fact that a developmental history exists does not rule out the influence of facilitating biological factors; these, however, are processed by and integrated into each individual's epigenesis in the spiral of his or her interactions with the environment. This manner of looking at the situation is coherent with Freud's conception of an etiological equation in which, in order to lead to the same outcome, the less constitutional factors there are, the more factual and historical ones are required, and the less factual and historical factors there are, the more there has to be of constitutional ones (Chiland, 1976).

All kinds of possible biological factors are being researched, involving genes, brain structure, cerebral asymmetry, and hormones (especially *in utero*); twin studies are being undertaken, with comparisons being drawn between homozygous and heterozygous twins and siblings; family history is being looked into, as well as sibling sex ratio and birth order.

Only a small number of brains have been available for *post mortem* examination, and conclusions are often drawn simply with reference to animal experiments. It is impossible to draw conclusions concerning human beings based on research done with rats for example—we would find it extremely difficult to describe the sexual fantasies of rats and their feeling of belonging to one sex rather than to the other.

From time to time, headlines in the press proclaim the fact that "the gene" of homosexuality has been discovered, the "gay gene" as Dean Hamer and Peter Copeland (1994) put it. Although Simon LeVay and Dean Hamer (1994) accept that no single factor can determine so complex a behaviour as sexual attraction, they do maintain that cerebral structures and genes (a plurality of genes) play a primordial role. These genes are said to create a certain degree of sensitivity. But the point remains as to what exactly constitutes sensitivity in a situation such as this. In addition, we must remember that the word homosexuality covers a whole range of phenomena: fantasies, acts, exclusive homosexuality, bisexuality, a phase in life— as in rituals of initiation (for example in Ancient Greece, in the Sambia studied by Gilbert Herdt and Robert Stoller (Herdt, 1987; Stoller & Herdt, 1990) and in the Baruya studied by Maurice Godelier [1982]). It should be noted, too, that almost nothing is said about female homosexuality.

The study of the pedigree of homosexual men leads LeVay and Hamer to attribute more importance to the mother; they have localized a marker at the extremity of the long arm of the chromosome X in the area Xq28. It would require a geneticist to discuss this finding and its implications in detail; as far as I am aware, this research has not been replicated, although similar studies might well exist.

The authors do, however, modulate their findings by recognizing that genes predispose to a particular sexual orientation rather than determine it. Genes code for proteins through RNA, and not directly for behaviour, still less for feelings.

Even if we accept that there are dimorphic cerebral areas, any blueprint that considers the male brain to be different from the female and the homosexual's brain to be different from the heterosexual's makes far too generalized a claim. Dimorphic areas may well control physiological reflexes and perhaps even specific behaviour patterns; but this in itself tells us nothing about complex feelings or sexual orientation. A homosexual man need not inevitably be impotent with women; *a fortiori* a bisexual man. One's biological equipment develops and is deployed in interactions with the environment; for human beings, "environment" includes relationships with key figures in one's life and one's cultural background; the end result is a unique individual history.

Studies of sibling sex ratio show that homosexual men have a greater number of brothers than heterosexual men, and that boys with gender identity disorder have significantly more brothers than sisters. There is also the impact of birth order, with homosexual men having more elder brothers than controls. It has been suggested that "with progressive maternal immune response to male Y, there is a posited disruption of the developing male's typical brain pattern of psychosexual development" (Green, 2002, p. 471). This hypothesis has yet to be satisfactorily proved. Anyway, the psychological links between siblings may play a role.

The tone of the debate is passionate. Homosexuals would like some biological explanation or other to be discovered: any reference to psychological factors is experienced as an attempt to make them feel guilty.

But no biological predisposition can come into force independently of some degree of interaction with the environment. There is a psychological "bedrock" just as much as there is a biological one: early psychological interactions may lead to certain characteristics that are just as difficult to mobilize as are their biological counterparts. The individual is no less innocent as regards the early psychological influences he or she has been subjected to as with respect to his or her genome or intrauterine life.

Even if there were some degree of biological facilitation, choosing the sex of one's partner remains a complex phenomenon involving cultural factors and one's personal history, as is the case with every complex psychological phenomenon.

Heterosexual and homosexual itineraries

Each of these itineraries has to be understood.

Heterosexuality is apparently straightforward enough—indeed, the English word *straight*, as applied to heterosexuals, emphasizes this: being "in line", "in order". Heterosexuality does not mean "normality", even supposing that something called normality actually exists; even though we never speak of normality nor think in terms of normality, our patients are forever asking: "Am I normal?"—a man unquestionably potent finds his potency insufficient, a woman who experiences orgasms does not recognize them for what they are: an orgasm must be much more sensational than *that*. I have already said that such individuals are comparing their own situation to what they had imagined about the giants of their childhood, the "primal scene" parents.

Of course we cannot avoid acknowledging that the complementary nature of genital configuration means that heterosexuality is part of "the order of Nature"; furthermore, only heterosexual intercourse can result in procreation without the assistance of medical techniques.

But, as I have pointed out, sexuality in human beings is separate from procreation because of the loss of *oestrus*, which exists in all other female mammals. Following Freud, our conception of human sexuality includes infantile sexuality, which has no procreative aim, and perverse sexuality, which is also dissociated from procreation and which was not rejected by Freud as being foreign to sexuality in human beings.

For a psychoanalyst, heterosexuality is the way of resolving the Oedipus complex that integrates both psychic bisexuality with respect to sexual orientation (love for the same-sex parent and for the opposite-sex one), and psychic bisexuality as regards identification (characteristics that have masculine or feminine connotations in our culture) in a gender identity that is relatively free from conflict. If the vicissitudes of one's relationship with one's parents are too great, this itinerary will be distorted; it can be difficult to discover these in some cases.

Sometimes people talk of heterosexuality or homosexuality as if it were a typical feature of one's identity, in other words a permanent one. If someone like John Money includes choice of partner as an aspect of gender identity, this is because he considers that gender identity in the fullest sense "without transposition" includes heterosexuality (1986, p. 105). There are various degrees of transposition, and some would argue that transsexualism is an extreme form of homosexuality, while homosexuality is a minor form of transsexualism. Identity transposition is at its maximum in transsexualism, in which the individual concerned wants to be "transformed" into someone of the opposite sex; it is visible, although to a lesser extent, in effeminate male homosexuals or masculinized female homosexuals. But in very "virile" gays and very "feminine" lesbians, if transposition exists, it is not apparent in any outward manifestations of their identity. As a consequence, the term "inversion", formerly the fashionable way of designating homosexuality, is no longer employed; even if the "invert", with a sexual partner of the same sex as himself, did not rebel against his identity and his appearance was unambiguous, it used to be said that he had the soul of one sex imprisoned inside the body of the opposite sex. This today would seem to be typical of those transsexuals who demand sex reassignment through hormones and surgery. Modern vocabulary is more precise in that it distinguishes between sexuality and sex or gender, and between problematic sexual issues and disorders of gender identity.

The burning issue of homosexuality

How are we to think about the observations that we make without hurting anybody's feelings? Although we must be careful not to exclude or condemn anyone, does this imply that we should turn a blind eye to certain problems?

The terms *homosexuality* and *homosexual* are offensive to those directly concerned. When they refer to themselves, they prefer to use words—even if they carry more opprobrious connotations—such as *gay* (which originally meant prostitute) or *lesbian*. Appropriating insulting terms in this way has been compared to the assertion of their "negritude" by Blacks referred to as "Negroes".

Is homosexuality an appropriate term anyway? It was invented by a Hungarian, Karoly Maria Benkert, who was known as Kertbeny, in 1869. It has been criticized because of its hybrid Greek and Latin origins. It has been suggested that the word homosexuality should be replaced by homoeroticism, the term used by Sandor Ferenczi, or by homophilia. From the perspective that I have adopted—highlighting the existence of two currents in sexuality, the tender one and the sensual or erotic one—it would be preferable to keep the term homosexuality to refer to the question as a whole, and to be specific about what we mean when we use the word: tenderness, sensuality or both. We could then use homophilia to refer to the feelings of tenderness and homoeroticism to refer to erotic acts.

There are different forms of homosexuality just as there are different forms of heterosexuality. The fact of being homosexual is not sufficient for characterizing someone in all of his or her aspects. As to the aspects that are shared by all the possible forms, how can we apprehend a sexuality that is practised with a same-sex partner? "Homosexuality has been called among other things a sin, an illness, a way of life, a normal variant of sexual behaviour, a behaviour disturbance and a crime" (Bullough, 1979, p. 1).

The idea of *sin* echoes the position adopted by various religions: Christianity, Judaism, etc. It could be thought that this standpoint should concern only the followers of one or other of these religions. But in our Judeo-Christian culture, the shared consensus is to a great extent contaminated by a conception of sexuality that judges it to be essentially impure and acceptable only in so far as it leads to procreation. The problem is not that homosexuality is considered by other people to be a sin, but that a certain number of homosexuals, whether they seek specialized help or not, experience it as such.

An *illness*? The American Psychiatric Association voted in 1973, by a majority of some 60 percent, to cease considering homosexuality as an illness. In so doing, the psychiatrists expressed the unease they felt, but of course solved nothing: is it conceivable that a show of hands can decide whether tuberculosis or measles is or is not an illness?

A *way of life*? Is it part of one's private life, or is it looking for public status such as the one that used to exist institutionally for the Berdache,[1] now fast disappearing. Or is there a double demand: to be recognized publicly and considered to be equivalent in every respect to the other way of life that is recognized by the laws governing marriage and family affairs?

A *normal variation in sexual behaviour*? In France, ever since the Napoleonic Code, if one's sexual life remains private and concerns consenting adults, the law does not interfere; in other countries the situation may be different—for example, in the United States, there are states which condemn fellatio and sodomy, even when they are part of the sex life of a lawfully-married couple (Harvard Law Review, 1990, p. 9–10).[2]

A *disorder of sexual behaviour*? For some homosexuals, homosexuality is ego-syntonic and does not generate internal conflict. Others experience it as not being *normal*. A therapist does not have at the back of his or her mind the idea that such-and-such is or is not normal; it is the patient who raises the subject of normality. The question arises not simply because norms exist, whether based on statistical or ideological considerations, but because human beings create norms, and have to share their norms with others. Such a person finds it impossible to regard his homosexuality as a norm because he feels driven by it; he is not master in his own house, and it prevents him attaining other aims that he is pursuing, apart from any measure of social retaliation.

A *crime*? Nowadays the situation is not as it was in Oscar Wilde's day—but it is a problem if the partner is a child. No one doubts the criminal nature of such an act if the child is subjected to physical abuse that may lead to his being killed. In cases of sexual seduction alone, there is much discussion. I have heard it said "We loved that child, we offered him an interesting experience, at a time when he was abandoned and left to fend for himself". When does playing with sexual seduction turn into sexual abuse? If the child involved is five years old? And if he is within a month or so of being of age, whatever the exact age at which this is defined, is it a crime or not?[3]

Homophobia

Although the term homophobia is widely used, its meaning is not particularly clear. Weinberg invented the term; Laura Reiter (1991) prefers anti-homosexual prejudice, because the phenomenon has more to do with aggressiveness against other people than with a phobia. The term homophobia is used to designate "any negative reaction or attitude towards homosexuals" (O'Donoghue & Caselles, 1993, pp. 181); as a concept or a "construct", it is still in its early days (ibid., p. 194).

Those of us who live in France are lucky; it is a country that, at the dawn of the 21st Century, is more liberal-minded than certain others. More and more of us refuse to be governed by ideological rules without questioning their legitimacy. Why then does homosexuality make many of us shrink back?

Are we afraid of awakening sleeping dogs? What dogs might those be? Perhaps the psychic homosexuality of our Oedipus complex is not as well integrated as we thought. Perhaps we are afraid that the fantasies or dreams we had fleetingly might turn into a carnal desire demanding to be satisfied.

Do the typical modes of sexual intercourse in homosexuality stir up feelings of disgust in us?

Mutual masturbation? The problem is not specific to homosexuality. Everyday language is replete with ambiguity. The etymology of the word masturbation (from the Latin *manus*, hand, and *stuprare*, to soil) brings to mind both the hand and the notion of stain or blemish. Masturbation designates the fact of "arousing oneself sexually or causing (another person) to be aroused by manual stimulation of the genitals" (Concise Oxford Dictionary), yet in everyday use the term refers to a solitary autoerotic practice that is not necessarily manual. Why do we insist on calling *masturbation* the mutual caresses that each partner gives the other, whether the couple be heterosexual or homosexual? Up till now I have met only two people, Jean Belaïsch and Anne de Kervasdoué, who, like me, are sensitive to the detrimental effect that this way of talking may have, with its reference to soiling, in reactivating the masturbatory guilt that many adults have not managed to overcome. "This somewhat pejorative—at least to some people—way of referring to the caresses that two people in love give each other seems inappropriate. In our opinion, the word ought purely and simply to be banished from our vocabulary." (Belaïsch & de Kervasdoué, 1996, p. 285, 292)

Nor are fellatio, cunnilingus, and anal intercourse specific to homosexuality. The term sodomy places anal intercourse under a shroud of disapproval even for heterosexual couples.[4] Each person does the best he or she can to overcome the barriers of modesty and distaste.

Even if we use only neutral terms, the idea of sexual intercourse between same-sex partners tends to make us shrink back. This may be because we are faced with two sorts of fear, both of which we have to cope with: the idea of sameness frightens the homophobic, while the homosexual is afraid of otherness.

In general, as far as sexuality is concerned, each of us is searching for reference markers; in our innermost being, sexuality remains a mystery to us. We strive to liberate ourselves from the pressures of our cultural group, whatever its nature. Heterosexuality leads to the possibility of having children by natural procreation and as a result finds itself on the side of the majority: it is necessary for the survival of the species. As Vern Bullough puts it (1979, p. 52, 62), although homosexuality may always have existed, it has never held a pre-dominant position anywhere. An exclusively homosexual social group would perish. Homosexuals are in a minority position and they quite legitimately claim not to be treated as an oppressed minority.

Fantasies, acts, identity and status

Do fantasies and ideas on the one hand, and acts on the other, lie on the same continuum, or is there a clear break between fantasy and action? Do isolated experiences have the same impact as a habitual mode of sexuality?

We all have had homosexual fantasies and desires—at least, this is the psychoanalyst's point of view. Sometimes actual homosexual behaviour can take place.[5] In the United States I have heard people say that a person who has had a homosexual fantasy (and a fortiori who has performed some homosexual act or other) *is* a homosexual; this would seem to indicate that, in the heterosexual community, there are vast numbers of frustrated homosexuals . . . unless the point is to exaggerate the number of homosexuals by fabricating thwarted heterosexuals.

This brings us back to the question of whether or not choice of partner is a fundamental part of one's identity. The fact is that someone whose object choice is heterosexual would never think of declaring his or her choice of partner, as we state our name, sex, age, national ID number, and so forth—all items of information that do not depend on us—or as we declare our faith, what we believe in. Proclaiming one's identity as a homosexual is an integral part of a militant combat against discrimination; we may believe it necessary to assert the immutability of homosexuality, to maintain that it is a biological characteristic, and to give it the same status as an ethnic difference, protected by law against discrimination. As Janet Halley points out in her well-researched and very subtle papers (Halley, 1989, 1994), claiming immutability is not a necessary factor in the struggle to obtain rights, and biological components are no longer accepted in any definition of race.

In the United States, discrimination exists in a way that has no equivalent in France. Here, no one would ask a candidate for a job, in the course of an interview or by means of a questionnaire, with whom he or she has sex; something which is common practice in the United States. This may explain why the fight against discrimination in the United States often takes the form of militant declarations made publicly.

There comes a decisive moment in the lives of those who are convinced that their sexual desires are exclusively or preferentially homosexual in nature and who have chosen to practice what they desire. That moment is when they publicly accept themselves for what they are, they no longer try to hide, they come out of the closet, out of obscurity, out of anonymity; "coming out" has connotations of "avowal" and of "liberation", both of which are more forceful than simply "saying it out loud".

Where do we draw the line between private and public life? Of course, when a man and a woman marry, among other things they are announcing the fact that they are going to have (or going to go on having) sexual intercourse together; and it is well known that, according to canon law, a marriage that has not been consummated may be annulled. There is nothing, in France, to prevent an adult man or woman having, in private, sex with any consenting adult partner he or she may choose.

Public declarations of homosexual choice include the wish to make society acknowledge the fact that such an option is in every respect similar to a heterosexual one. The aim, inter alia, is therefore to obtain official recognition of same-sex unions, the right to marital status, and the possibility of being the co-parents of a child.

Cultural change is sometimes strange in its effects: in many heterosexual couples the partners live together, have children, get on well with each other and have no intention of separating—but they do not marry. Marriage as an institution could well be suppressed and replaced by two kinds of contract, one applying to situations in which people live together and the other relating to reciprocal parental rights and duties when children are born of that union.

Same-sex couples demand the right to marry, rather than simply to have official registration of partnership or of mutual assistance contracts: marriage opens up the possibility, for a male-female couple, of becoming the co-parents, through adoption, of a child and allows the spouse to have access to medically-assisted procreation (in France, surrogate mothering is prohibited by law).

Allowing homosexuals to be considered as the co-parents of a child would be a turning point that many of those who have thought deeply about the question would find difficult to accept. Irène Théry (1997) emphasizes the symbolic value of recognizing, when it comes to lines of descent, the existence of two sexes and the difference between them; Daniel Cohn-Bendit (1998) highlights the importance for a child of having both a father and a mother, and any child psychiatrist could only support that point of view. Nobody would dispute the fact that homosexual parents are perfectly capable of bringing up children in a loving atmosphere. The only issue is that of recognizing two men or two women as the child's *two parents*.

To have a child is presented as being a right, whereas in fact it implies a commitment and a heavy responsibility—even though many parents are not initially aware of that, even though some may procreate "inadvertently". In the desire to have a child, there is both an object-related component (a child for him- or herself) and a narcissistic one (a child for oneself). It is quite obvious that the narcissistic component is very much to the fore in homosexuals—but, then again, they are not alone in this. When people are able to procreate by themselves, they do not have to justify anything; when the *socius* is asked for something, it grants itself the right to examine any matter it feels important.

We could discuss at length the fact that children need both a father and a mother, and the unfortunate consequences that the lack of one or both parents may bring in its wake. As far as medically-assisted procreation is concerned, the CECOS (*Centres d'Etude et de Conservation des Œufs et du Sperme*—Egg and Sperm Research and Preservation Centres) hesitate; when they were created, ethical rules were drawn up, and they consider artificial insemination by donor to be a gift from one couple to another couple. As I write, adoption has taken on an entirely different meaning: it is no longer a question of finding a home for abandoned children, but of finding children for childless couples—who go far afield to find them and are willing to buy them.

Male and female homosexuality

Homosexuality in men and in women ought not to be seen as symmetrical, just as male and female genitalia are not symmetrical. It is noteworthy that much more has been written about male homosexuality than about its female counterpart.

In their childhood, women have a very close physical and emotional relationship with their mothers. Later in life, women tend still to share tenderness, kisses and complicity in their relationships in a way that men do not. Men come together to share actions, in a spirit of sporting or military fraternity; although physical contact is not excluded, it is not of the same order.

Male homosexuality has a different history: it has its place in Greek mythology, a role in the *paideia*, the upbringing of ephebes; it has a part to play in initiation ceremonies in certain cultures (New Guinea). On Lesbos, Sappho had her institution for young girls, but this is an isolated example; female homosexuality plays no part in Greek mythology (Sergent, 1996), nor in the upbringing of women in ancient times.

When the aim is to draw up prohibitions against homosexuality—for example, in biblical or theological texts—the concern is mainly or exclusively with male homosexuality. Often female homosexuality does not even rate a mention. The only thing that counts is sperm, and throwing away one's sperm is disapproved of: Onan (Genesis 38, 7–10) is condemned for refusing to inseminate his sister-in-law, the wife of his deceased brother, by withdrawing during intercourse (not for having masturbated, as the term "onanism" might lead one to believe). Homosexuality is an even more clear-cut case of wasting one's sperm and avoiding procreation.

There have, of course, been situations in which women have shared very close intimacy—in the *gynaeceum*, in harems and, in modern times, in the hammam. In cases of homosexuality *stricto sensu*, the sharing of tenderness plays a significant role; homosexuality is not reduced to being a purely sensual affair, as is the case with certain kinds of compulsive male homosexuality, in which the aim is to find a new partner every day. For some women, their homosexual union comes after an initial heterosexual one; the male partner did not provide them with the tenderness they find with another woman.

Female homosexuality arouses a particular kind of curiosity in men. In pornographic films, there are few scenes of homosexual intercourse between men; scenes in which women have sex together are constantly being shown, not in order to discover how they make love "because they have nothing with which to do it", but out of fascination with the internal hidden part of women, out of a desire to divest them of the power they supposedly possess, and out of a wish to degrade them.

In contemporary gay culture in the United States, the most typical and traditional meeting place for homosexuals is the gay bar (and this obviously engenders a high level of alcoholism), according to Douglas Carl (1990)—with no hint of disrespect because he is himself homosexual and a practitioner of systemic therapy for same-sex couples. For Carl, group sex is a much more common activity in homosexual men; in general, women's sexual habits are much more private. He maintains that women prefer to get to know a possible partner and only later have sex with her. In *The Homosexual Matrix*, Tripp (1975) emphasizes the fact that on average the men in the study had had sex with a hundred partners, most of them anonymous, whereas the women had had, on average, ten partners, who in general were known to them.

The lesbian movement is different from its gay counterpart in that the women involved are above all committed to fighting for women's rights.

From the outside, it is difficult to imagine just how much the gay and lesbian world has grown. There is a true gay and lesbian culture characteristic of our contemporary world. The need for procreation has become less of an obligation now that infant mortality has been reduced. Individuals demand the right to have the freedom to indulge in their own pleasures. Were there as many homosexuals in former times, though they did not "come out" because of the persecution to which they were subjected? Or is it that gay and lesbian culture generates vocations?

Homosexuality as initiation

It is practically only for men that homosexuality appears, in mythology and in reality, as an initiation serving as a prelude to entry into adulthood. For women, of course, there was Sappho, who ran an establishment for young girls on Lesbos; and in New Guinea, young women suckled the breasts of older women in a kind of initiation ceremony that, was, however, nothing like as important or as lengthy as the initiation ceremony for men.

Here again, as I have emphasized throughout this book, it is absolutely crucial not to consider women's sexuality and gender identity as symmetrical (all other things being equal) to those of men.

The first observation that should be made is that, in cultures where men and women are much more separated in daily life than in our society, a male infant belongs above all to the world of women: he is nourished at his mother's breast, he sleeps by her side, and he is surrounded by women. There comes a time when he will be separated completely from her—torn from her—in a painful experience that nothing will soften; on the contrary, in fact—it is almost as though he had not only to leave his mother but also to get rid of any hint of her femininity that she might have communicated to him. The woman on whom one has depended so intimately is dangerous; she has to be demeaned as much as possible in order to protect oneself from her.

As a young man reaches puberty, his initiation by an adult is intended to enable him to become a hunter and a warrior, a man capable of accepting full responsibility as a member of that community. This aspect of *paideia*, education or upbringing, is discussed openly, but we are often much more discreet when it comes to the sexual relationship between the *eromene* and his *erastes* (the term pederasty is evocative of this . . .). In fact, we do not have as much detail concerning how the ancient Greek or Indo-European societies functioned as we have for the tribes of New Guinea. Ethnographers have lived with the Sambia (Herdt, 1987) and the Baruya (Godelier, 1982), they have witnessed initiation ceremonies, and some have even been initiated themselves. What they tell us, however, tends to remain at the level of reported facts. All the same, Herdt tells us of the emotional shock that he felt in experiencing the actual situation, even though he had been told of the secret practice of homosexual fellatio: "[T]hree months later, in the privacy of ritual initiations, when I saw the secrets become flesh in florid and open homoerotic play, I was astonished and embarrassed." [Stoller & Herdt, 1990, p. 42]

This is a socialized and ritualized form of homosexuality that combines homoeroticism and homophilia; in addition to the pleasure inherent in the act itself, more emotional relationships spring up between partners who choose each other. This homosexuality lasts only for the duration of the initiation rites; when the time comes, it gives way to heterosexuality and to marriage. Furthermore, not every kind of homosexual act is authorized (and indeed ordained): there is no question of mutual caresses or anal intercourse, only oral intercourse is tolerated. This is an illustration of the importance given to sperm, which a man cannot produce if he has not himself already received some. In the first two phases of the initiation ceremony, boys between 10 and 13 years of age, still pre-pubertal, have to suck the penis of young unmarried men and swallow their sperm. In the third phase, when they are between 14 and 16 years old, they themselves, henceforth pubescent, will be sucked and will give their sperm to the young initiated of the first two phases. In the fourth phase, the young man is officially married and initiated into the secret rites of men. Genital intercourse with his wife does not take place until the fifth phase, after his wife has had her first period. Sex with her is initially oral: the man has to inseminate her for her to be able to produce milk (the reader will notice in passing how the woman is deprived of a function albeit specific to her sex). The sixth phase occurs when she becomes pregnant for the first time. Full adulthood is achieved only when the couple have two children.

Herdt's in-depth interviews allow us to see from the inside what some of the Sambia people feel about this experience. The young boy must first be forced to take part in the initiation ceremonies; he does not want to leave his mother and spend the rest of his life in the men's quarters. He feels no immediate pleasure in sucking another man's penis and in swallowing his sperm. Later, he becomes somewhat more knowledgeable, and chooses to sleep with one person rather than another; later still, when the time comes for his penis to be sucked, he will prefer some boys to others. In each phase, the roles are not interchangeable, and the prohibitions against incest have to be respected: this is the case in particular for brothers, less so for cousins. The homosexual partners, far from being close to each other, are in fact potential enemies. Among men, sex is an erotic game; with a woman, it is work, and the production of children depends on it.

Homosexuality takes place in a context in which beliefs and practices are quite clearly defined; not everything is permitted, and individual pleasure and choice are possible only within fixed limits.

Fellatio between men, a representation that in our culture may generate feelings of disgust leading to homophobia, is here simultaneously an obligation and a pleasure, while other forms of homoeroticism are excluded.

This detour via the Indo-Europeans, Greeks and Papuans has taught us that homosexuality and homophobia depend on the cultural context in which they appear; that we can neither justify nor condemn them on the grounds of human nature; and that, if institutionalized homosexuality does exist, there is no society in which homosexuality is practised to the exclusion of heterosexuality— simply because this would mean that the social group itself would face extinction.

The couple

Unless one takes a vow of chastity and is married to God, the desire to form a couple, the desire to be desired and loved, is a line of force in the life of every man and woman. The life-span of a couple may be short and dominated by sensuality; it may be long-lasting and governed by social rules, while at the same time—this is one of the paradoxes of our culture—being the fruit of choice and of romantic love.

The idea that one may remain unmarried is completely foreign to some cultural traditions; others do not even contemplate that it could be possible to choose his or her partner. In western society, our point of view—at the beginning of the 21st Century—is distorted, because we live in a world ruled by laws on monogamy (even though the kind of monogamy of which the law has cognizance has little to do with actual social *mores*) and suffused with the "romantic" yearning for a union based on love; this yearning is fuelled by beautiful myths and by literature, and it heads more often for failure than for triumph.

Marriage is an event that concerns society. The economic aspect of marriage is less important nowadays than it once was; in so-called primitive societies, the division of labour between the sexes necessitated a family unit comprising men and women (men hunted, while women did the crop-picking). Nowadays, the family is no longer a unit of production but a unit of consumption; each individual, whatever his or her sex, can obtain the foodstuffs necessary for survival and carry out the simple tasks of everyday life. Communication and relations between families are looser and are not ritualized. The constraints set up by the incest prohibition, which in certain societies give rise to highly complex rules and regulations, are reduced to a minimum: no spouse is prescribed, and only a limited number of marriage unions is completely forbidden (father or mother and child, brother and sister). Other prohibitions (uncle and niece, aunt and nephew) may be lifted by special dispensation. The question arises as to why people still get married—many couples live together, have children, have no inclination to separate, yet do not marry (or marry much later on). One could say—jokingly, of course, but only just—that those who defend marriage are first and foremost those who do not have access to it: Roman Catholic priests and homosexuals. For priests, marriage would mean recognizing their right to sexual life; for homosexuals, it would imply recognizing the normality of their sexuality.

Since the aim of marriage is to found a family, it necessarily implies sexuality. The link between sexuality and love is typical only of a limited number of societies, including our own. In situations where marriages were decided without taking the individual persons and their feelings into account, love—or hate, for that matter—could find itself tacked on . . . Nowadays partners choose each other, love is there at the beginning (but is often lost as time goes by); the result, as far as happiness is concerned, is not always convincing. Choosing a spouse involves affinities that have to do with social standing, upbringing, and, as I have said, corresponding elements in each person's lovemap. Given that life expectancy is longer than in former times, each spouse continues to follow his or her itinerary, and it can happen that spouses do not always develop in the same way.

In France, an adult is free to do whatever he or she wants in bed with any other consenting adult. The law intervenes only in cases of violence or when a minor is involved. Incest is not prosecuted as such, the relationship between perpetrator and victim being simply an aggravating circumstance in cases of rape or sexual assault. Sexuality is less "regulated" than in many so-called primitive societies, where sexuality outside the bonds of marriage usually has to follow the rules laid down by the prohibition against incest. This is the case for pre-marital sex, more widespread than in our culture, and for extra-marital sex, which is not always permitted. In such societies, the modalities of sexual intercourse are defined more narrowly than in our culture.

Monogamy as the law defines it concerns simultaneous unions, not successive ones following on death or divorce. Roman Catholicism prohibits even divorce. In India, there was once a custom according to which a widow had to throw herself on her husband's funeral pyre. Yet at the same time some compromise has to be reached with "[the] deep polygamous tendency, which exists among all men". (Lévi-Strauss, 1949; 1969, p. 38)

Only on rare occasions has that tendency led to institutionalized polygamy. In fact, when we talk of simultaneous multiple marriages (polygamy), we really mean *polygyny* (a man having more than one wife), because *polyandry* (a woman having more than one husband) is extremely rare. Where polygamy is legal, the womenfolk manage as best they can. Principal wife and co-wives are sometimes supportive of and helpful towards one another. But it can happen that they hate and try to harm one another. Institutionalized polygamy means that women available for marriage are much fewer in number, and some men resort to official homosexuality. Evans-Pritchard (1990) studied an ancient custom among the Azande of southern Sudan: while a man was a warrior in a battalion of unmarried men, he would take a *boy-wife*, because the rich noblemen had monopolized all the women, installing them in their vast harems. The warrior thus had a male partner who would satisfy his sexual needs (resorting to adultery was excluded because of the extremely severe sanctions it entailed) until such time as he could marry a woman. This homosexual union was a temporary affair; the boy-wife carried out for his/her husband the everyday tasks ordinarily reserved for women, and this situation was considered to be a *learning period*.

If we cast our eyes around, we would see that polygamy is *widely*—indeed *officially*—practised: the legal wife, together with any co-habitees and the children of these various unions, are all present at the funeral of their deceased partner, even when the latter was a member of the social elite. Some feel indignant, others take it to be proof of open-mindedness. It would seem, therefore, that although polygamy may not be legal, it is not only widespread but also officialized.

Over and beyond the question of polygamy, society's ambition to regulate sexuality by law, religion, moral codes, etc. is a success as regards some aspects, but a failure as regards many others. The tension between prohibition and desire is unrelenting—indeed, it could be said that, for some people, prohibition fuels desire. Sometimes transgression ends in tragedy, sometimes it is tolerated in all of its vagaries.

As regards children, the law has certainly moved on: children born out of wedlock and adulterine children now have rights, and they are beginning to free themselves from the opprobrium of which they were unjustly the target—for they are in no way to blame for what their parents have done. Children born of an incestuous relationship, however, are still in a twilight zone.

As is well known, the law with respect to divorce has changed considerably. Spouses who separate create a painful situation for any children they may have—even though it is better for them to separate than to tear each other apart. Many children live more or less simultaneously in two "reconstituted" families.

And if we were jackdaws . . .?

Let our thoughts wander for a moment or two . . . How simple things would be if we were jackdaws, as Konrad Lorenz describes them (1949)! These black birds, a species of crow, choose their partner for life (and they live a long time); and even though they have not been formally married by the local registrar or by a priest, they remain perfectly faithful to each another.

Human beings torture themselves in many ways. Sexual diffe-rence plays a part in this, because adapting to the opposite sex implies that two different sensualities and two different sensitivities have to find a common meeting-ground. Obtaining the greatest possible satisfaction implies *intimacy*, something that a couple can attain only when there is mutual penetration of body and soul. This in turn implies that it is not meant for show nor to be displayed in public.

During a *Gay Pride* demonstration, I heard homosexuals say: "We want to be able to kiss each other in the street". Heterosexual couples, of course, do kiss in the street without being booed, but these public hugs and kisses are not the best thing they do and are completely irrelevant as far as the solidity of their relationship is concerned. By definition, intimacy belongs to the private, not to the public, sphere.

Some people reach orgasmic pleasure easily, but it leaves them with feelings both of emptiness and of depersonalization: the term "little death" is apposite here, as is the phrase *post coitum omne animal triste est*. A man and a woman, strangers to each other, lie side by side, with each of them wondering what they are doing there. Or the feeling of letting oneself go is perhaps so intense that it leads to blurring of the body's frontiers and a fear of depersonalization.

Being mentally at one with each other changes the nature of the "afterwards" experience. But deep understanding alone, without sexual satisfaction, is not enough for creating a happy couple. Here again we find the union between sensuality and tenderness in sexuality.

Living together day after day erodes passion; each has to be very tolerant of the other's peculiarities, a great deal of patience is called for, and the word "compromise" is often mentioned. Could we imagine Romeo and Juliet as an elderly couple, in their sixties, for example? Of course, there is always Philemon and Baucis . . .

There are strange things about the way sexuality functions in human beings. An unmarried couple, for example, are happy in their sex life, as in their everyday life; after marrying, with the reactivation of unconscious conflicts and the Oedipus complex that marriage entails, things begin to go wrong between them.

This is the point at which we come up against "neurotic prohibitions", which are not of the same nature as the prohibition against incest. Only once in our professional life, perhaps, will we be consulted by patients in direct difficulty over the incest prohibition— for example, a brother and sister couple, who had lived together for many years and had had children, were living abroad and wanted to return to France, but they were troubled by the fact that they would not be able to marry and officialize the status of their children. On the other hand, we are consulted almost every day by patients who do not succeed in making love to their partner or spouse—who is not a blood relation, nor a relative by marriage, nor in any way prohibited by law. Their partner is neurotically prohibited, in terms of their Oedipus complex, because he or she is too like (or too unlike) the patient's father or mother, and associated with painful conflicts in the patient's past. The Oedipus complex and the social prohibition against incest are not isomorphic; there is a connection that has to be understood between what lies at the origin of the social law and what leads people to accept it, and between social regulation and the distorted imitation of it offered by the superego's prohibitions.

The desire to live as a couple makes for distress in same-sex couples, when no place is assigned to them in the fabric of society. Homosexuals do not demand special status like that of the Berdache, the Hijras, etc. They do not want to be treated as a third sex or a third gender, they want to be treated like everyone else. The tenderness that unites same-sex couples is perhaps to be understood as a need for reparation with respect to something that is felt to be missing in their childhood relationships with their parents.

On that point, Moberly (1983) has suggested an interesting hypothesis. She thinks that the desire for a sensual relationship with a same-sex partner hides a desire for what I call tenderness. The homosexual suffers from an attachment disorder with respect to the same-sex parental figure. It has sometimes been said of male homosexuals that the father has been too absent and the mother too present in their life (the same is said of male transsexuals). Moberly is more subtle; she argues that the father may well have been present and done everything possible for his son, yet the son still felt deprived in some way, as though what he had received from his father was felt to be insufficient. According to Moberly, the only way homosexuals can be helped is through repairing the relationship with the same-sex parent. This point of view is, to my mind, innovative and corresponds to my own clinical experience.

Men and women tend towards union, yet so many obstacles hold them back. The complementarity, as well as the difference, between their genitals brings them together, puzzles them, worries them. Another person has to be discovered; their experience of their own body cannot serve as a basis for understanding that other person. It is easy to imagine that homosexuals have the impression that they understand their partner better, because they can feel in their own body what their partner feels. However, opposite-sex partners may also manage to identify with each other without feeling threatened as to their own identity, and to be attentive towards what goes on inside their partner and what can satisfy his or her desires. No truly happy couple can exist without each partner respecting the other as an independent person with his or her own desires, desires that have to be taken into consideration.

Notes

1 The Berdache are a social institution, widespread among North American Indian tribes and in Siberia. Men dress in women's clothes (or, sometimes, in special clothing) and live like women; many of them are shamans.

2 In 24 states and in the District of Columbia, sodomy was still a crime in 1990, when the Report was being drawn up. Under the general term sodomy, the law forbids both ano-genital and oro-genital contacts. The 24 states, from North to South and East to West of the United States, are: Alabama, Arizona, Arkansas, Florida, Georgia, Idaho, Kansas, Kentucky, Louisiana, Maryland, Michigan, Minnesota, Mississippi, Missouri, Montana, Nevada, North Carolina, Oklahoma, Rhode Island, South Carolina, Tennessee, Texas, Utah, Virginia. In Massachusetts, anal sex is punished only when it does not involve consenting adults in private.

3 The problem of defining and establishing the limits of sexual abuse exists also for heterosexual acts.

4 Once again, Belaïsch and de Kervasdoué (1996, pp. 286–287) write with much tact and sensitivity; something I have not seen in other authors.

5 Kinsey, who was not a psychoanalyst, wrote two reports that support this view.

CHAPTER SIX

Sexual wanderings

T hey say that happy people have a pretty uneventful history; stories about happiness do not interest or excite people. What, then, *does* excite people? The sheer intensity of our instinctual drives, their "essential violence"? The erotic drive or the destructive one? One author who has written more than most about "sexual arousal", Robert Stoller, says: "I do not know what libido is", and claims that this is even more the case for the death instinct (Stoller, 1991a, p. 4). Yet he does say that *hostility* is part of arousal; perhaps that is another way of expressing the fact that some sort of balance has to be found between Eros and Thanatos. We are not governed by drives that head directly towards their aims. Now that it is dissociated from the aim of procreation, the sex drive wanders about restlessly but forcefully in search of satisfaction. It finds what it is looking for either with another person or in opposition to that other person.

For arousal, there are products (books and films) called *erotic* and others called *pornographic*. Where does the frontier between eroticism and pornography lie? It has been said that today's pornography is tomorrow's eroticism.

Is there a discrete gap between imagination and realization? Does what we imagine open the way to carrying it out, or does it enable us not to have to?

There is another frontier that is sometimes mentioned: that between consenting and non-consenting individuals. Does this frontier, mentioned by Stoller a propos of sado-masochistic acts, apply to prostitution?

In the quest for sexual paths which divert from "ordinary" life and which lead to "extra-ordinary" drive satisfaction, it becomes difficult to treat the other person involved with respect. Everything it touches is degraded—the man, and especially the woman (who may even be reduced to slavery by her male partner), and sexuality itself. The couple is replaced by partner-swapping and sexual frolicking with several participants, intimacy is replaced by voyeurism and exhibitionism.

In discussing these wanderings, it is impossible to avoid the term *perversion*, even though the concept does give rise to a number of difficulties.

The first and most important of these lies in the derogatory overtones of the word itself. The second has to do with the distinction between perversion and perversity, to which terms there corresponds a single adjective, perverse. The third is the problem of the relationship between perverse fantasies and perverse acts. The fourth lies in the connection with cultural tradition: there is no universally valid definition of perversion. The fifth has to do with the fact that when we speak of perversion we are usually referring to men; what is the situation of women with respect to perversion?

Perversion, rejection and sin

The Latin verb *pervertere* means "to turn about, to overturn"; perversion is a "deviation", a "distortion or corruption", an "alteration from the original course" (Oxford Dictionary), "a change from better to worse, a degrading" (Lanteri-Laura, 1978). The term is suffused with moral reprobation and rejection.

There was no rejection in the way that Freud treated the problem; in this, he was a true revolutionary as compared to the previous century. For Freud, perverse sexuality is part of the sexuality of human beings. What enabled him to reach that conclusion was his fundamentally developmental conception of sexuality. A child discovers the erogenous zones one after the other (oral, urethral and anal, genital), explores them and manipulates them; they are sources of pleasure. Children like to exhibit themselves and try to see how others are made. They are curious about the relationships that adults have; whether or not they succeed in seeing what goes on between their parents, they construct a sado-masochistic fantasy based on their experience of their own body and on what they may have seen animals do—this is what we call the "primal scene". Freud was later to acknowledge that sexuality in children is less exclusively auto-erotic than he had first thought in 1905; but it does not include full sexual intercourse with penile intromission and the possibility of impregnation. In adolescence, when full sexual intercourse does become possible, the nature of the relationship with the other person changes. Henceforth, sexuality will be under the pre-eminence of the genital zones and of object-relations. The infantile sadistic and masochistic elements will have to be integrated into relationships with others.

Freud said that children were *polymorphously perverse* because, throughout the normal stages of development, there are mani-festations of component instincts and of tendencies that are found in all sexually-perverse adults: Freud interpreted these in terms of fixation at, or regression to, infantile patterns. Perverse sexuality is no more than an exaggerated version of infantile sexuality broken down into its particular tendencies.

However, some children are more "perverse" than others, with manifestations that are anything but discreet. What should we think of the 6-year-old boy who, in the initial consultation, drew a little boy sucking at a little girl's genitals? Later, we learned that he did indeed treat the little girls in the apartment block where he lived in that manner. What are we to think of boys (girls are somewhat of an exception here) who torture animals, pets or not? This acted-out sadism in childhood is not a good omen; it is not infrequently found in the background history of adults who commit sexually violent acts (Balier, 1997).

"No healthy person, it appears, can fail to make some addition that might be called perverse to the normal sexual aim; and the universality of this finding is in itself enough to show how inappro-priate it is to use the word perversion as a term of reproach." (Freud, 1905d, p. 160). Freud is here speaking about normality, which he defines as the highest point of development; he does not treat it qualitatively as a different way of being or of expressing one's sexuality.

The involvement of the various erogenous zones is part of what are usually called "preliminary" pleasures—kissing, for example (which, in fact, is not practised in every culture). Freud was particularly revolutionary when he wrote that any form of intercourse can become part of a couple's sex life as long as it is not the inflexible and exclusive condition for having pleasure, and if it acknowledges and respects the otherness, the desires and the personality of the partner (primacy of the object-related aspect). Perversion begins where there is exclusivity, inflexibility, absence of respect for the other person and demands for his or her unconditional surrender. In the strict sense of the word, perversion should apply "only to [the] extreme instance" of "humiliation and maltreatment of the object" (Freud, 1905d, p. 158).

With the term sodomy are associated homosexuality and violence. Sodomy is used to designate anal intercourse in general, but it ought to be reserved for cases in which violence plays a part. In his writings, Sade[1] groups together homosexuality, paedophilia, incest and coprophagy,[2] and expresses the horror that the female genitals arouse in him. This is what the women locked up in the castle of the *120 Days of Sodom* have to do (1998, pp. 72–73): "You feel [. . .] the risk there is in cooling down the mind of a libertine waiting, I suppose, for an arse for his discharge and to whom some imbecile presents a cunt. In general, offer yourselves very little by the front; remember that that revolting part to which Nature in her folly gave shape is always the one that is the most repugnant to us." "Offer yourselves" is a strange way of putting it, because there is no freedom of choice, only coercion and punishment in case of disobedience: "Remember that it is not at all as human creatures that we look upon you, but simply as animals that are fed for the service we hope they will render us and that are thrashed if ever they refuse to render it." Sade himself, in fact, uses the word "perversity" in his writings.

Education and perhaps development itself build barriers of modesty and disgust. If they do not relax somewhat, sex could never be a very happy experience. *Inter faeces et urinas nascimur*, we are born between faeces and urine. The female genitals are situated between the urinary and the anal orifices, and from there flows the blood of menstruation. The penis discharges urine and sperm.

Breaking down these barriers in the way sado-masochistic acts do is to deconstruct the body, including the frontiers between inside and outside. In addition, it destroys the value of pain as a signal showing that protection is required against aggression and danger.

Stoller (1985, p. 4) makes a very eloquent development of the overtones of rejection inherent in the word perversion: *"Perversion is so pejorative. It reeks of sin, accusation, vindictiveness, and righteousness. [. . .] There is little to the word but insult: hostility that aims to humiliate and subjugate others. As a label, it has been a power tool used by society to transform those who are different into those who are bad."*

Stoller suggests that perverse acts and sin should be linked together. "Everyone knows that the concept of sin is at the center of the word *perversion*. [. . .] It may be unscientific to believe in sin, but it is also unscientific to believe that people do not believe in sin. [. . .] *The activity is perverse*, I shall say, *if the erotic excitement depends on one's feeling that one is sinning."* (Stoller, op.cit., pp. 6–7)

Sade certainly had that feeling when he spoke of impurity while at the same time declaring himself to be a libertine. Being a libertine in the sense in which Sade used the term is far removed from what many of us would call "freedom of thought", the fruit of inner processing and integration that enables us no longer to need religion as a protection against the fear of death, for example. Sade's intention was to mock religious symbolism—for example, by trying to force a woman to have an enema then to throw up over a crucifix. This was not a fantasy that could be enshrined in literature, but a fact reported by a woman, part of a series of cruel acts for which she filed a complaint; Sade was found guilty and sentenced to a term of imprisonment.

In Stoller's writings, the feeling of sinfulness appears less brutal and less grotesque. For him, the basic idea is that of "harming", "harming someone", humiliating the other person in an attempt to render null and void the humiliations suffered in childhood and transform them into triumphs. Perversion has to do with the individual's past history, and as such can be accessible to insight and to attempts to change things. Sade does in fact acknowledge that there is a link with his existence (his past history) and with his "organization" (his constitution); but he doubts that any change may be possible—in fact, he does not want to hear of change: "With some systems that are very much attached to their existence, especially when one has sucked them in together with milk, it is never possible to give them up. [. . .] Morals do not depend on us, they have to do with the way we are made, our organization." (Lély, 1982, pp. 339–40)

"My manner of thinking stems straight from my considered reflections; it holds with my existence, with the way I am made. It is not in my power to alter it; and were it, I'd not do so . . ." (ibid., p. 348)

The distinction between perversion and perversity is a question that is always being raised, without any satisfactory answer ever being given. Sexual perversion is evocative of a particular kind of orgasmic pleasure, while perversity involves treating other people in a purely destructive way. But when the object, thanks to whom sexual satisfaction is obtained, is degraded, "humiliated and maltreated" (to use Freud's words), fetishized and dehumanized, is the wandering, the deviation or the departure from the ordinary limited to the sexual sphere?

Even though we may be concerned to eliminate any a priori moral disapproval, it is difficult to do away with the term *perversion*. Joyce McDougall writes of *neo-sexualities*; in so doing, she moves away from the idea of perversion as "simply a regression", Freud's position, or a "deviation". Her aim is "to highlight the innovative dimension of these erotic inventions" (Fine, Le Guen & Oppenheimer, 1993, p. 147). Others continue to use the term perversion, while emphasizing that they are refraining from any moral judgement. This is the position of Estela Welldon, who has written a remarkable book on perversion in women (Welldon, 1988); she prefers the term "perversion" to that of "deviation", which implies only a statistical anomaly. Perversion is a clinical entity describing cases in which the individual does not feel free to reach genital satisfaction, but is subjected to a compulsive form of activity in which unconscious hostility gradually gains the upper hand.

Perversion: differences between men and women

The psychoanalytic theory of sexual perversion focuses to a considerable extent on fetishism. As a result, men have the monopoly of sexual perversions. The fetishist can have an orgasm only in the presence of the fetish, which represents the penis that his mother and all other women do not possess; at one point in his childhood he noticed that his mother did not have a penis, and this observation generated in him a high level of castration anxiety—which he attempts to deny by creating a fetish. Some authors have tried to show that women can have fetishes too (Zavitzianos, 1982), representing not the mother's penis but the father's; this hypothesis, however, is not particularly convincing.

Furthermore, men again are in the majority as far as sado-masochism is concerned. In his "ethnographic" investigation of those who organize and frequent *Bondage and Discipline* establishments, Stoller (1991a) reports that clients who resort to such services are almost exclusively male.

Why should only one half of humanity—the male half—be perverse, or at least more perverse than the other half?

For Stoller, one possible reason lies in the particular set of problematic issues that a boy has to cope with: having had to separate from his mother, he experiences "symbiosis anxiety", against which he defends himself by perversion. The reader will recall that perversion always involves denigrating women.

The assertion that sexual perversions are essentially a masculine preserve ought to be nuanced: fetishists and sado-masochists find partners who submit to these acts; even though they may not initiate the process, the latter agree to participate in the "perverse scenario".

However, if perversion does exist in women, it has to be looked for elsewhere. Estela Welldon has shown this most clearly. In women, perversion is expressed by the body as a whole (anorexia, bulimia, self-mutilation) and by child abuse. The aim is different too: in men, perversion is directed towards an external part-object; in women, towards their own body or objects they consider to be of their own making—babies, treated as part-objects. While men assert themselves in a *locus* that is external to them, the importance for women of an "inner space"—much more real than a missing penis—has to be taken into consideration. This inner space is the *locus* of pregnancy and childbirth, breast-feeding, all the parts of a woman's anatomy that are linked to fullness, warmth and generosity.

That is the level at which a mother may abuse her child. Janine Chasseguet-Smirgel (1984) has described in many of her writings the role played by the mother of the perverse adult when he was still a boy—arousing and enticing him while he was still sexually immature.

A girl who has been abused by her mother repeats that aggression, particularly via prostitution. Any woman who, as a former victim of maternal ill-treatment, of sexual abuse or of incest, turns to prostitution deserves all the sympathy we can give her.

Prostitution

The importance of sexuality is such that men are prepared to pay for sex in circumstances where, generally speaking, only the sensual demands are satisfied, tenderness being absent or reduced to a minimum: what is this irrepressible need? Men pay, and women, whether they are manifestly obliged to or without any obvious constraint (but here the whole idea of consenting to prostitution would have to be debated), agree to sell their genitals, a private part of themselves, to a whole series of men. What paths in life have been followed by women who end up in this "prostitution of sexuality" (Barry, 1995), this degraded form of sexuality?

Here again we come across one of the leitmotivs of this book: the asymmetry between men and women, the differential valence of the sexes. Although prostitution involves both men and women, it is mainly women who are prostitutes even if nowadays, in certain places, one-third of all prostitutes are men[3] (Welzer-Lang, Barbosa & Mathieu, 1994); it is mainly men who are procurers, although some brothel-keepers are women. The clients are almost exclusively men; a few women resort to a gigolo or male escort, but there are no men who offer themselves to women in the street nor—generally speaking—male brothels for women clients, although the Bulloughs mention that an establishment of this kind did exist in Hamburg in 1972.[4]

In addition to the double set of moral standards, the asymmetry characteristic of the sexes as regards prostitution has certainly to do with "the sexual difference". If a woman can turn a hundred "tricks" a day in rapid-turnover brothels (she does not have to feel desire or pleasure), a man cannot "shoot his load" a hundred times a day (even though some pornographic film actors boast of being able to have an erection whenever they want, the length of the refractory period is still a factor); a brothel in which men offered themselves to women would not have the same turnover or be as financially profitable an undertaking. A man's desire is different; the "urgency of stiff cocks", to use Stoller's expression (1985, p. 35), is acknowledged to be irrepressible and legitimate. A woman's desire has more "romance" attached to it, and was for a long time either denied or acknowledged simply in order to repress it (this went as far as sexually mutilating her: the clitoris, source of pleasure, had to be excised).

How, deep in her soul, can a woman manage to put up with the fact of being sold or of selling herself as a mere sexual commodity? If we exercise our minds, we may be able to imagine the situation: it is not simply a matter of overcoming the barriers of modesty and disgust erected during our upbringing. Over many years, Kathleen Barry collected information from prostitutes all over the world; she writes of the four stages of dehumanization that a woman goes through:

- Distancing herself from her own being, her identity as a person;
- Emotional disengagement (she has to force herself not to have any feelings);
- Dissociation (henceforth she is simply three holes into which men empty themselves);
- Disembodiment and pretence (cut off from her body, she acts the part expected of her and pretends to experience sensations and feelings).

In Vietnamese, prostitutes are called "girls with torn-apart entrails" (Nguyên Du, 1961). It is not in the least difficult to imagine that women need alcohol or drugs in order to put up with what they are going through; some too are drug addicts who are forced into prostitution in order to pay for their addiction (Hermann & Rieck, 1978). As a result, some women find themselves in deep despair; many of those who become human wrecks, homeless and destitute, were victims of sexual abuse and incest in their childhood. Prostitutes live in constant fear of being assaulted, and some do end up being killed. Migrant women, lured by deception, are particularly at risk. There is a considerable trade in women from the Far East and from those countries that used to be on the other side of the Iron Curtain (Legardinier, 1997).

What paths in life must a woman follow for them to lead her to prostitution? The distinction between so-called "free" and "compulsory" prostitution is untenable. A woman who thinks she has made a free choice when in fact she was led to prostitution by a history of childhood abuse, poverty and unemployment is only deceiving herself, even though she may not have a procurer. In fact, most female prostitutes are controlled by pimps (this is not the case with male prostitutes), and are subjected to extreme forms of violence if ever they try to free themselves from him and get out of prostitution. It is misleading to claim that a prostitute willingly hands over money to a man: "And what if I like being beaten up . . .?" Is the "consent" given to a pimp who seduced her, made her love him and promised her the earth, really a well-informed decision made voluntarily, in other words true consent?

Gail Pheterson (1989, 1996) is undoubtedly a charming and generous person,[5] but I cannot agree with her when she defends the right of women to be prostitutes or militates in favour of prostitution being recognized as a profession just like any other. She is quite right to insist that prostitutes be recognized as human beings, but selling one's body is not a job just like any other. As Kathleen Barry pointed out in her first book, published in 1979, it boils down to the prostitution of sexuality itself, it is degrading for the women involved, and it reduces women to the status of slaves.

Prostitution is quite rightly condemned as being the major form of sexual exploitation of women by men—exploitation not only by the procurer but also by the client. What needs are there in men that must be resolved by resorting to prostitution? Who are the prostitutes' clients?

For the past two generations in France, most young men do not have to be "initiated" in a brothel (Spira, Bajos *et al.*, 1993), the result both of a transformation in the sexual life of adolescents and of the disappearance of double moral standards with respect to this. Few parents are so recalcitrant as to oppose the new-found freedom that today's adolescents have; if they do, a breakdown in relationships between them and their children is the usual outcome. Adolescents of both sexes thus discover sexuality together. There are still a few young men, however, who do resort to a prostitute. Some of them, in my experience, suffer from serious mental disorder and are incapable of establishing a relationship with young women in their immediate circle.

Some men are impotent with women whom they admire and respect, like their mother and sisters, and succeed in having sex only with prostitutes. This is part of clinical reality, and Freud clearly saw the importance of it for understanding how the mind works: in men, the split between Madonna and whore is always ready to emerge or to re-emerge. Such men, however, do not represent the majority of those who frequent prostitutes.

In our culture, the situation is different from what it used to be elsewhere, when adultery was punished so severely that a man who resorted to prostitutes was typical of men who remained unmarried through no fault of their own (the age at which marriage was authorized; polygamy in which a few men monopolized all the women) or of sexually-frustrated married men. It has been said that prostitutes play a part in maintaining a certain equilibrium in society by facilitating social stability and domestic peace. "Go and see a whore," says the wife who finds her husband's sexual demands excessive. Although she may *say* this to him, it is by no means certain that she will not blame him later if he acts on her suggestion and does indeed go to see a prostitute . . .

Man's polygamous appetite is satisfied if he resorts occasionally or regularly to the services of a prostitute. Prostitutes may also offer him "special satisfaction", the kind that he would not dare ask of his wife or that she refuses to give him: fellatio, anal intercourse, sado-masochistic acts. Perversion and prostitution go hand in hand. In prostitution, kisses are not part of the contract, in which each part of the body, each hole, each "speciality" carries a price-tag.

It is thought justifiable for men separated from their wives by incorporation into the armed forces or by economic migration to resort to prostitutes. Military brothels are organized affairs. Migrant workers are the clients of the "rapid-turnover" brothels, where they have only a few minutes in which to "empty themselves". Some clients interviewed by Welzer-Lang, Barbosa & Mathieu (1994, p. 126) spoke of their need to "empty their balls", to "find a hole", to "shoot their load". "Hanna Olson has described male sexuality in prostitution as 'male masturbation in a female body'" (Barry, 1995, p. 34). There is no place in any of this for a true human relationship or for any tenderness whatsoever.

Things are not the same with regular clients. Some prostitutes "claim that their role is that of a therapist, of an ancillary welfare worker, almost of a social worker" (Welzer-Lang, Barbosa & Mathieu, 1994, p. 166). Of course a certain hierarchy does exist in the world of prostitution, from the lowest *pornè* of ancient Greece, the prostitute who works in today's rapid-turnover brothels, to the highest *hetaira*, the courtesan or mistress in former times, the modern Japanese geisha or female escort. Some women have thereby climbed the ladder of social hierarchy and have married important personalities. It is with reference to such women that some writers have spoken of a "career" in prostitution (Corbin, 1978; Adler, 1990): prostitution is a career when social advancement enables the woman to leave it behind.

The industrialization of prostitution, the trade in women, the situation in Thailand, the Philippines and elsewhere, sex tourism—all condemn women to an extreme form of psychic misery. And no-one appears to feel indignant about it unless children are involved. Above a certain age, women are deemed to have consented, even though in fact they have been completely misled as to the fate that awaited them.

Society cannot ignore prostitution, even if it is only to the extent that it may involve a public health problem—the spread of venereal disease: formerly gonorrhoea and syphilis, now the dreaded AIDS (some clients ask for unprotected sex). This public health issue has led some countries—France in the past, Germany today—to *regulate* prostitution. It is not at all obvious that regulation would solve the public health problem; on the other hand, it would constitute an official acknowledgement of prostitution, and lock women into their fate as soon as they register. The United States (at least in some states) has given up the idea of *prohibiting* prostitution as it did alcohol, and for the same reasons: it is ineffective, and it opens the door to a take-over by organized crime. In France the solution presently adopted—abolishing regulation—does have weaknesses: it decriminalizes prostitution for the prostitutes themselves, but it does lead, if not to legal endorsement of prostitution, to a de facto acknowledgement of it via the fines imposed by the police for soliciting (soliciting is prohibited, not prostitution) and the income tax that prostitutes are required to pay (yet they have no social security cover . . .). Procuring is condemned by law; some people want clients to be condemned also.

The quasi-universal existence of prostitution has led to its being accepted with resignation even by people like the Bulloughs, who have denounced the fate to which women are subjected as the "subordinate sex" (Bullough, 1973) and stigmatized the double set of moral standards that apply in this domain. There was a time when nobody imagined that one day slavery or apartheid would disappear (true, they have not entirely disappeared, but some decisive steps have been taken towards that goal). Feminists make a political analysis of prostitution, which they see as resulting from male sexual domination; they believe that a struggle is necessary if women are to obtain the human rights that are denied them in prostitution. The change in the status of women has already made for a change in *mores*, and this can only accelerate. Removing the guilt attached to masturbation, and the decrease in young men's initiation in brothels thanks to the evolution of adolescent sexuality are examples of ways in which sexuality can be satisfied while respecting women. Prostitution never respects the dignity of women.

And yet prostitution is still being presented as a profession (Adler, 1990, p. 12); "the oldest profession in the world". The *oldest*? Many other professions are at least as old. But, first and foremost, is it a *profession*, a profession like any other? Ought not this *trade* be abolished, since it trades in the human body (though this kind of trading is not prohibited everywhere in the world)? As I have said, some feminists—Gail Pheterson, for example—believe that prostitution can be a profession and demand that prostitutes' rights should be upheld by organizing prostitution differently, not by its abolition.

Objections expressed in some quite concrete ways highlight the paradox that lies behind the wish to consider prostitutes as "sex workers". Lydia Bragiotti, co-ordinator of the "Women's Bus" in Paris, says: "It's a profession, because you have to learn how to do it, but it's not a profession because no-one wants his or her daughter to take it up." (Welzer-Lang *et al.*, op. cit., p. 9). Again, some have argued: "If prostitution is to become a profession, it would logically have to figure in Job Centre adverts and training seminars would have to be organized. Are we ready to accept what that kind of choice implies?" (Mouvement du Nid, 1987, p. 5)

There are therefore two contrasting points of view: on the one hand, prostitution is considered to be an offence against the dignity of the prostitute as a person and a degradation of sexuality, an infringement of women's human rights; on the other, it is claimed that one can prostitute oneself with dignity, and that all that needs to be done is to re-organize the profession so as to give prostitutes the same rights as all other workers. These two points of view are nonetheless in complete agreement over their refusal to stigmatize people who are prostitutes: they are above all women who live under duress, who suffer, who struggle to bring up their children and who are particularly helpless as old age approaches. Their disagreement concerns the issue of stigmatizing prostitution as such.

Strangely enough, in the fight against procuring, those who try to help a prostitute find themselves a little too quickly accused of pimping—for example, it is impossible to let an apartment to a prostitute or to put her up without being suspected of procuring, thereby making her attempt to break free of the trap she is in all the more problematic. Conversely, powerful pimps, members of the Mafia and organized crime, manage never to be brought to justice.

In this domain as in so many others, there are in our modern world a handful of men and women dedicated to helping women and men break free of prostitution, while at the same time others, more powerful thanks to their wealth and their connections, weave the net in which they entrap and ensnare their victims.

Pornography

The word first appeared in French in 1769, as "the pornographer" in a text by Restif de la Bretonne, with the etymological meaning, from the Greek *pornographos*, of "writing about prostitutes". The modern meaning of the word is somewhat different.

Whatever the medium chosen (text, image, film, viewdata service, Internet, etc.), pornography consists of "printed or visual material containing the explicit description or display of sexual organs or activity, intended to stimulate erotic rather than aesthetic or emotional feelings" (Oxford Dictionary). Not all explicitly sexual material has this aim: for example, textbooks on sex education are intended to inform and no more. Anything may stimulate erotic excitement and be used, for personal purposes, as pornography. The content of this kind of material merits a much more detailed description.

We could try to draw a frontier between erotic and pornographic. Erotic material does not resort principally to homosexuality, incest and what Freud called component instincts (oral, anal, voyeuristic/exhibitionistic, sadistic/masochistic)—those that are not subject to the primacy of the genital zone and are not object-related; pornography makes use of all of these. Erotic material does not convey a degrading view of women and children, subjecting them to the will of men; pornography does. The degree of hostility and destructiveness is not the same; in Stoller's words (1970, p. 490): "No victim, no pornography". As Stoller points out, hostility is one of the essential dynamics of pornography; sexual arousal, especially in men, requires a certain degree of brutality and hostility. It is true to say that, more often than not, the ordinary consumer of pornography is a man; the kind of pornography that women indulge in involves schmaltzy novels that appeal to sentimentality as a means of fuelling their sexual excitement.

By that yardstick, some books that claim on first sight to be erotic ought to be considered pornographic. Even though the *Story of O* was written by a woman, it tells the tale of a woman reduced to slavery; although this may well give her pleasure, she is still the victim of male domination and cruelty. Her consent only goes to show how alienated a woman is when she thinks that, if she is to keep the love of the man she loves, she has to accept absolutely everything. Perhaps, in an exaggerated way, this is the story of so many women . . .

As regards pornographic material itself, a distinction should be made between what is written text and what is presented as images. A written page leaves room for the imagination, so that individuals can represent things in any way they may choose. An image that reveals everything leaves little room for fantasy.

An individual may write or draw something, and that something will be the product of his or her imagination; but beside that, there is what is *enacted* in a video or a film—and *that* is the product of a lucrative industry requiring producers, agents, scriptwriters, directors, and actors who will "go live" and sell their body and their genitals just as in prostitution, especially in hard-core films where scenes are not mimed but actually carried out.

Pornography does not restrict itself to heterosexual genital intercourse; among its essential elements, as I have stated above, are what Freud called component instincts: oral, anal, voyeuristic/ exhibitionistic, sadistic/masochistic. These component instincts are not subject to the primacy of the genital zone, nor are they object-related, hence the connection I have mentioned with perversion in Freud's definition of the term. The fact that past humiliation may seek revenge via this kind of material helps establish a link with what Stoller defines as perversion. It has to be said once again that whatever is experienced in the intimacy of a loving relationship between two people takes on a whole new dimension when it is put on display to an external observer.

Every one of us has experienced the situation in which an image or a story that someone else would find ordinary or lacklustre is enough to trigger an erotic arousal. This is the case even when we are not particularly trying to find some material that would arouse us sexually.

It is too often the case that, before (or instead of) being able to discuss pornography and think calmly about it, we (ourselves or others) are overwhelmed by subjective, emotional and defensive responses and by moral concerns. Yet we must try to think about it, because pornography does exist: it involves a limited number of perhaps unusual people, writers and actors, producers and distributors, all of whom participate in what is called the pornography *industry*—and it involves also a vast number of consumers. The fact is that pornography is widespread—yet, as Gérard Vincent points out (1987, p. 379), "Though sex-shops and cinemas that specialize in X-rated films may do a roaring trade—and they do—we do not see queues lining up or crowds flocking to their doors".

Who participates in the pornography industry? What drives people to become consumers of pornography? Is pornography dangerous, neutral or beneficial?

Stoller, the only psychoanalyst to have conducted "ethnographic" research into pornography, may offer us a glimpse into the pornography industry and its members; his investigation was limited to pornographic films and videos, which Stoller calls "porn", to distinguish them from other pornographic material. He did not actually witness porn being filmed or recorded, but conducted interviews in his consulting room, listening to what was said with the ear of a psychoanalyst. It took him many years before he could make contact with the men and women of this somewhat peculiar world. In his books, Stoller (1991b, 1993) reports these interviews as they were recorded, with a bare minimum of editing. It should be added that all the interviewees read his reports before publication; this is standard practice in the United States, and Stoller has always done everything he can to follow that rule. He thus allows us to respond freely to the practically raw material that he collected.

In the years when I was a member of the Cinema Control Commission, commonly known as the "Board of Censors"—although the commission itself rejects that term—I was constantly asking myself a question that apparently interested nobody but me: who are the actors and actresses who agree to being filmed in sex scenes, particularly in hard-core films where such scenes are not make-believe but are actually carried out, with camera shots from all angles to ensure that the minutest of details can be seen? Stoller answers that question, at least in part.

Among those who are exclusively actors/actresses, the women agreed to be interviewed by Stoller while the men refused. Stoller emphasizes the great variety in their personalities: there is no typical profile of the porn actress—they range from the "hysterical and histrionic" woman to the one who has become head of a company specializing in porn and is particularly elegant in appearance, with, somewhere in between, the nurse who, living a double life, comes close to the category of "multiple personalities". Some marry and raise a family. Some were professional actresses who found in porn the "stardom" they had been unable to obtain in mainstream Hollywood. For others, making money more easily was their main motive. A few manage to become actresses in mainstream Hollywood productions; others stay in the porn business doing other things.

Bill said that he "existed for glory and immortality" (Stoller, 1991b, p. 32) more than for anything else and that he had found them in the porn industry, where he began as an actor, then moved on to being a scriptwriter, a director and an agent. His father died when Bill was four years old, he *rebelled* against everything his mother wanted to such a degree that he was admitted to a Juvenile Hall under a care and protection order, and he stayed there from age 12 to 16. He liked it so much that he later returned to the home to work as a specialized youth leader, identifying with the "kids" and always taking their side. His porn actors are also like "kids" to him, and he treats them like those in the Juvenile Hall. He does not live like an adult belonging to the adult world. He has no wish whatsoever to toe the line and start a family. He talks (boasts?) about his performances on the film-set: he is a sex animal, his penis is exceptionally long, "I am a piece of meat" (op. cit., p. 49), he can have an erection whenever he wants and can copulate several times at a stretch. On the set, he enjoys his power and can "choreograph" his orgasms (op.

cit., p. 50), thus enjoying them better than in his private life; he is adulated by the audience. In Bill's opinion, those in the pornography business are in porn because they were "repressed" in their childhood. According to him, some porn actors feel wretched and are on the brink of suicide—they do it only for the money—while others enjoy what they do. As to the spectators, Bill thinks that porn is "a masturbatory aid first and foremost" (op. cit., p. 61). He states quite plainly that many porn films are boring and poor quality productions in all respects (this was exactly my view too when I was a member of the Cinema Control Commission).

The question of the harmfulness of pornography is constantly being raised. All the investigations I have read indicate that, for the most part, public opinion is not or is no longer hostile to the distribution of pornographic material when it involves adults (Diamond & Dannemiller, 1989); any material that presents and therefore involves children is condemned. It is extremely difficult to decide what kind of role pornography plays, cathartic or harmful (McCormack, 1988). It has been claimed that pornography may be informative. According to Money [1988], videos and *Jack and Jo* clubs (for homosexuals) can play a preventive role with respect to AIDS; the idea is to watch a film in which gay men have sex, while masturbating alone or with a partner; the spectators can thus become experts in manual activity without exchanging body fluids.

There is no direct link between watching porn and committing sexual assault. More specifically, in the case of paedophiles (Howitt, 1995), watching a porn film is not necessarily a prelude to actual assault; on the other hand, all the sex offenders studied by Howitt had been sexually abused in childhood by adults or by peers older than themselves. The review of the question published by Fukui and Westmore (1994) failed to establish whether or not pornography in a purely erotic form had any harmful effect whatsoever on human behaviour.

That said, violent pornography has been claimed to influence people (Cramer & McFarlane, 1994); violent pornography reinforces men's belief in the "myth of rape": "women always want sex and say no only to entice". In a sample of 87 women who had been physically assaulted, Cramer and McFarlane found that 40% of their partners whlized violent pornography and 51% of them were influenced by it.

Wandering to the point of losing oneself

All of us wander here and there in our appetite for sex until we find what satisfies us. "All erotic desires are aberrant," writes Stoller (1991a, p. 35), who draws the conclusion that the term "normal" should be unequivocally banned. More often than not, the sado-masochists he interviewed for *Pain and Passion* did not appear to him to warrant a psychiatric diagnosis.

We are all mad to some extent, and all perverse to some extent. But there is all the same a difference between those who wander about so much that they end up losing themselves, and those who find a road that will lead them to pleasure and intimacy with no need for fetishes, sado-masochistic acts, degradation of their partner or criminal deeds. The frontier is not easy to trace. Our private madness and our private perversion may help us not to condemn other people out of hand and to treat those who come asking for assistance. Being a psychoanalyst means acknowledging the fact that our patients' childhood history has contributed to their wanderings; but we cannot help those who ask nothing of us.

It is true that, to some extent, we can encourage them to seek help. Claude Balier and his team, for example, working in a prison environment (1988, 1996) within a regional medico-psychological unit, succeeded in bringing male prisoners accused of assault (sexual and non-sexual), or already serving their sentence, to seek treatment. This kind of experience is quite unlike a psychoanalyst's ordinary practice and demands a great deal of the professionals involved. Balier suggests a category he calls "sexual perversity", distinct from perversion in the wider sense; the patient may end up murdering his victim "in order to avoid a psychotic catastrophe by temporarily limiting his very existence to the instinctual drive itself and its activation in the environment". In that process, neither the object nor the self still exists as such.

Notes

1 The term sado-masochism is generally used, because the existence of a sadist implies that of a masochist who consents to being mistreated, and also because the same person may alternate between the two positions. However, one cannot but agree with Gilles Deleuze when he writes (in his Foreword to *Presentation of Sacher-Masoch*): "As soon as one reads Masoch, one feels very clearly that his universe has nothing to do with that of Sade" (1967, p. 11). The discussion I present in the following paragraphs applies to Sade's universe, not to that of Masoch.

2 There is so much dung and coprophagy in the *120 Days of Sodom* that even his biographer, Gilbert Lély, writing an apologia as much as a biography, felt discouraged and ended up talking of the "monstrously exaggerated space" that is given over to the topic (Lély, 1982).

3 Male prostitutes are not caught up in the procurer's net in the same way as women are; most of them prostitute themselves as "women". Some have serious disorders of gender identity and become prostitutes in order to convince themselves that they really are women, not simply in order to earn enough money to have an operation, as they claim to be doing (in France, the operation is paid for by the social security system . . .).

4 According to Vern and Bonnie Bullough, a brothel staffed by male prostitutes for women clients existed in Hamburg in 1972; it was called the Yellow House. When a "situations vacant" notice was published to recruit staff, some sixteen hundred men applied for the vacancies . . . No other information is given as to how this brothel functioned or what became of it. See Bullough & Bullough (1987, p. 302).

5 Gail Pheterson is co-director of the International Committee for Prostitutes' Rights (ICPR), which brings together prostitutes and non-prostitutes in order to defend the profession of "sex worker". At the time of writing [the original French version of] this book, she was a senior lecturer in the University of Amiens.

CHAPTER SEVEN

Love

If sex makes the world go round, and love is the greatest thing in life, in what way are love and sexuality connected? Nowadays we tend to call on three Greek words in order to express what we mean by love: Eros, Philia, and Agapè. Could this be an attempt to distinguish between three forms of love by opposing them, to look for a delicate balance between three sorts of demand, or to prepare a subtle elixir with three ingredients?

It is easy to see the link between Eros and sexuality, but less so a priori when it comes to Philia (friendship) and Agapè (Christian love). Yet the most sublime or sublimated forms of love have their roots in the flesh—every human being has to have a body, a history; everything begins with his or her conception and birth, and growth continues throughout childhood.

We could turn to literature and poetry, morality and ethics, philosophy and religion; but the starting-point I adopt here is that of clinical experience and the knowledge that underpins it. No human being is capable of love unless he or she has been loved. All love must integrate ambivalence.

Being loved in order to love

Everyone needs to have been loved in order to be able to love—to love oneself, to love another, to love one's neighbour.

In morals and religion, there is a commandment to love one's neighbour—even though, in other circumstances, it is readily

117

acknowledged that love is not something that can be commanded. The expression, originating in the Old Testament and taken up in the New—"Thou shalt love thy neighbour as thyself" (Leviticus 19: 18; Matthew 19: 19;/22: 39; Mark 12: 31; Romans 13: 9; Galatians 5: 14; James 2: 8)—properly understood, implies that God loves mankind; it is only because God loves human beings that they are able to love themselves and each other.

As I have said, I am considering these issues from a clinical point of view—which tells us that no child can develop without a minimum of love, and no child can go on developing without continuous tender loving care and attention.

Have we not always known this implicitly? Yes, if we think of everything that has been observed and said about motherly love, even if the poets go somewhat over the top . . .

"A mother's love—love no-one can despise:
Wondrous bread, which a god divides, yet multiplies!
Perpetual food in the parental hall:
Each has a share, and each one's share is all!"

In these lines, taken from "This century was two years old . . ." (in *Autumn Leaves* [1831]), Victor Hugo ignores the often intense and always present rivalry between siblings, which exists side by side with sibling complicity, of course, as a protection against parental severity.

That children need to be loved can be seen quite clearly in the fact that, in the days when they used to be packed off to the country to be brought up by childminders, they would die like flies. For a long time, people began to show interest in children only after they had survived the first few months of life, as though to protect themselves against repeated bereavements.

A child's need to be loved from birth onwards was turned into a scientific theory thanks to the pioneering work of René Spitz and John Bowlby.

Spitz used the term *hospitalism* to describe the distress experienced by children brought up in satisfactory conditions of hygiene and diet but who were not given the kind of affectionate care that a mother or mother substitute offers. Just before the outbreak of the Second World War, he compared children who, raised in a prison nursery, were in regular contact with their mothers, with children raised in an otherwise well-appointed nursery unit who spent their time lying in bed looking up at the ceiling (which was all they could see), with no stimulation and no individualized care. His attention was drawn to the manner in which children in this latter group just let themselves waste away.

Bowlby developed the idea of *attachment* to explain the distress he observed in children separated from their mothers, even if they were hospitalized for only a short time. He derived the concept of attachment from ethology: a young animal follows its mother in order to avoid predators; the aim of the behavioural system of attachment is to maintain the baby close to the mother and to adjust the distance between them. According to Bowlby, Freud's idea of the primary link between baby and mother involves nothing other than nutrition; however, when Freud speaks of the baby at the breast, he is not in fact referring merely to feeding and orality. He says that the infant at the breast finds in the mother's arms warmth, gentle rocking, caresses and *tenderness*. (On many occasions, Freud says that the baby is tenderly attached to the mother, *zärtlich gebunden*, tender attachment, *zärtliche Bindung*). "The person of the child's mother [. . .] not only nourishes it but also looks after it and thus arouses in it a number of other physical sensations, pleasurable and unpleasurable." (Freud, 1940a, [1938], p. 188). Bowlby keeps Freud at arm's length because he is critical of the concept of the reflex arc, the mechanism of discharge, preferring a cybernetic conception in which feedback plays a major role. But attachment is not in itself an anti-psychoanalytic concept, as some have argued, and Bowlby, himself a psychoanalyst, was close to what is known as the object-relations school of thought: the instinctual drive searches not for satisfaction but for the object. Once we emphasize that drive satisfaction is obtained via an object and not by means of a simple mechanical discharge, the distance between Freud and Bowlby is much less.

Harry Harlow (1971) reared young macaques under experimental conditions in which, separated from their mother, they had access to different substitutes: a wire-frame mother holding a feeding-bottle, and a mother with no feeding-bottle but covered in soft fur. The baby monkeys spent more time on the furry mother than on the wire-frame one, even though the former did not have a feeding-bottle; according to Harlow, this proves that the primary link is not nutritional. Under natural conditions, a mother has fur (or a soft skin) and breasts, and a baby who was looking simply for fur would die; in fact, babies have a "burrowing" reflex that causes them to search out the breast and helps them find it. Harlow shows also that young monkeys prefer a warm substitute to a cold one, and one that rocks gently to an immobile one; this corresponds to Freud's description of the mother as a source of warmth, rocking and caressing her infant.

Harlow showed too that when an animal reared without its mother becomes an adult, it is incapable of mating—and that the peer group can play a major role in mitigating this failing. It is rare for human children to be abandoned completely to their own devices, with no adult presence. This was, however, the case with the Bulldogs Bank Children (Freud, A. & Dann, 1951), who lived in a concentration camp from when they were just a few months old until they were over three years of age; they managed to survive and to create some form of mind-structure thanks to the mutual support that they gave one another via primary identification with the *socius* rather than with the absent mother.

More and more research is becoming available to show the consequences of ill-treatment and abuse of children: an open door to many kinds of pathology and delinquency. One of the paradoxes—and by no means the least—of these situations is the child's attachment to abusive parents: a bad object is better than no object at all.

The capacity to love oneself, a felicitous form of narcissism, derives from what, with Winnicott, we would call "primary narcissism".[1] A good-enough mother provides her infant with good experiences. She offers her breast or the feeding-bottle more or less just as the baby begins to feel hungry, so that the infant does not become exhausted through crying—and in such circumstances, says Winnicott, the baby has the illusion of having actually created the breast or feeding-bottle and therefore of providing this good experience him- or herself. One day the infant will have to let go of this illusion, but it will have established a feeling of self-confidence in the child and formed the basis for the transitional space (cultural space) in which objects become meaningful not because of their material qualities but because their meaning is a shared one.

It is impossible to love another person without this basic self-confidence. Without it, we cling to the other person because we need to be repaired by someone. If ever that person weakens, we feel threatened and fall prisoner to "narcissistic defences", the primary aim of which is to protect and repair ourselves, not that of having consideration for the other person. Such defences are pathological; their deadliness is far removed from happy narcissism.

The inevitability of ambivalence

One important difference between Bowlby and Freud lies in the fact that, for Freud, object cathexis is always ambivalent whereas, for Bowlby and others who refer to attachment theory, only some forms of attachment are ambivalent.

The ineluctable nature of ambivalence results from Freud's final version of the drive theory, in which two classes of instinct, life instinct and death instinct, are distinguished. The death instinct is not understood in the same manner by all psychoanalysts; indeed, not all psychoanalysts accept it.[2] Freud sees in it an urge to return to the inanimate state; although we may continue to follow Freud in his clinical investigations, when he proposes the useful and thought-provoking concept of "defusion" operating alongside a "binding" element, we need not accept this "metabiological" speculation of his.

For his or her survival, the infant depends on someone else— usually an adult, if we leave to one side extreme and exceptional cases such as that of the Bulldog Banks Children. This experience of dependence may be a happy one, but it is never *entirely* happy. Infants have at some point to dismantle their illusion with respect to the feeling of omnipotence that they draw from the fact that food and other care seem to arrive exactly on time. The land of plenty, says Alain (1934), is an illustration of what infants experience in the early months of life, when they obtain everything they want as long as they utter the appropriate incantation. They will have to learn that nothing can be obtained by words alone; work, too, is required. Dependence is happy only during the phase that Winnicott called "double dependence", in which the infant is wholly dependent but is not aware of the fact. Becoming aware of dependence is a painful process. We do not have the object under our control, and we are always dependent on the love object. In order to maintain or to recover control, the loving link may even be attacked. The death instinct "is then called the destructive instinct, the instinct for mastery, or the will to power". (Freud, 1924c, p. 163)

Admitting the inevitability of ambivalence implies that we have to integrate it and overcome it, instead of letting it surge into surprising kinds of behaviour that are the very opposite of love.

We hate only what we love. The speed with which love switches to hate when the object does not meet one's expectations is well known. The sheer intensity of passion is devastating, as is its desire for control over the object. Juries, at least in France, show leniency towards crimes of passion, because they realize that, behind the murderous deed itself, lies a love that has been scorned.

Death and love are intertwined in the great romantic portrayals of love. The flame of love burns all those who approach it. It is impossible to imagine love's ardour dying little by little in the petty little conflicts of everyday life. Romeo and Juliet, Tristan and Iseult can only die young, and die of their love for each other.

Freud wrote of the narcissistic over-valuation of the object which, he says, characterizes the man's love of a woman but not the woman's love of a man. In every kind of love, in its initial stages, there is an over-valuation of the object. There may even be what I call "coat-hanger love": the demand to love and to be loved is so great that one "hangs" that love on to another person, whatever he or she may really be like—in fact with hardly a thought for what he or she is like—because of the urgent *hic et nunc* need for love. Even though we may pay a little more attention to the other person, we still cannot know what he or she is really like, because we are seeing that person as we would like him or her to be. If we manage to be slightly more perceptive, we imagine that the other person will change because of the influence our love must bring to bear. A beautiful but dangerous illusion: perhaps the other person *will* change, but the only happy love is one that is capable of accepting the loved object as a "package deal"—as that person really is, and not as we would like to make him or her become. When the idealized image is replaced by a more realistic one, the ensuing collapse may be highly unpleasant; hate lies in wait, lurking in one corner of a broken heart.

Pure love does not exist, only love that becomes purer in the course of one's life, thanks to trust, reciprocity and intimacy. The other person's concerns thus end up being taken into consideration in the same way as one's own are.

Transference love

With Anna O., one of Breuer's patients described in *Studies on Hysteria* (Freud, 1895d), Freud discovered transference love. All patients who visit a doctor, a fortiori a "doctor of the soul", psychoanalyst or psychotherapist, experience strong feelings stirring up inside them—hope (everything will become possible again) and apprehension (embarrassment or shame when they talk about secret aspects of their life). They end up loving their therapist without admitting it to themselves in so many words—indeed, they deny the very idea, unless they develop an "erotic transference" in which awareness of this love, its powerful nature and the desire to make it known come to the fore. Analysts see in the transference a repetition of the relationship with primary love objects, the patient's mother and father, with these parental figures being projected on to the analyst. What the parents had been unable to do, the analyst will have the capacity to accomplish. Thanks to his or her understanding and love, the analyst will be able to repair the patient.

The situation is a highly delicate one. Transference love truly is love, with its ambivalence, its demands and its vicissitudes. At the same time, it is a misleading kind of love. It is not the analyst as a real person who is loved (patients know very little about their analyst, even though in the course of an analysis they end up intuiting a great deal about his or her inner being), it is what the patient "hangs" on the analyst—this is the prototype of what I call "coat-hanger love". The difference with respect to coat-hanger love in ordinary life has to do with the analyst's response. In ordinary life, the loved person does not feel bound by any obligation as regards the one who has fallen in love—the importunate lover can be pushed to one side. Of course, if the loved person feels flattered by this love, he or she can keep it burning and thereby encourage the development of erotomania, the lover's passionate conviction of being loved in return. The analyst must neither push that love away, because it is "true" love and an important element in the treatment, nor respond to it as one would respond in everyday life. The response of the analyst who takes in, understands, and interprets (when it becomes possible for interpretations to be integrated), without falling inopportunely in love, makes "analysis of the transference" possible—with the patient gaining insight into what he or she is looking for in the analysis and in life itself. Falling in love in ordinary life also implies transference elements, but there the partner reacts in terms of his or her own needs, not from a perspective of understanding and "benevolent neutrality".

Transference love creates dependence and, as with all kinds of dependence, suffering. The greater the love, the greater the dependence and the greater the suffering. One has to be cured of transference love. Some say that the transference has to be "wound up". But no love can be wiped out without a trace. If those traces are to be beneficial, the "negative transference"—the hate, resentment, and envy that go to make up the ambivalence of transference love just as in any other kind of love—has to be clarified, interpreted and processed. Some patients run away when they first catch a glimpse of their negative transference; in such cases, the circumstances of their leaving are unfortunate. In the course of the analysis, patients ought to have managed to express their aggressive feelings and thus be able to leave without feeling crushed by a debt of gratitude that they cannot reimburse; that is why it is preferable for patients to pay their analyst. In the analysis, the analyst has placed him- or herself at the patient's disposal, without becoming directly involved in the patient's life or tying the patient down in any way.

In order to be able to "handle" things in this way and resolve the transference, the analyst must control the "counter-transference", the analyst's own projections with respect to the patient. The patient should not be expected to contribute anything to the analyst's own personal life, although, professionally speaking, patients do teach their analyst a great deal and enhance his or her skills.

Eros

It is because of the eponymous Greek god who appears in many myths and legends that Eros designates passionate love and uncontrollable sexual desire in all of its violence. "Eros was always considered to be a fundamental force in the world, even after the Alexandrian embellishments of his legend. He is the one who guarantees not only the continuity of the species, but also the internal cohesion of the universe." (Grimal, [1951], 1969, p. 147). Regarded at times as an omnipotent god, at others as a "demon" mid-way between god and man, the son of *Poros* (the Expedient)—like his father, he always succeeds in imagining some means of reaching his goal—and of *Penia* (Poverty)—like her, he is constantly searching for his object. Sometimes he is the son of Hermes and Aphrodite, or again of Ares and Aphrodite—and in this case he is called Anteros, contrary love. Poets see in him a winged infant whose arrows cause cruel wounds.

When Freud uses the word Eros, he is indeed referring to sexual love as well as to the internal cohesion that Pierre Grimal mentions. The German language has just one word for all forms of love: *Liebe*. Freud writes:

"The nucleus of what we mean by love naturally consists (and this is what is commonly called love, and what the poets sing of) in sexual love with sexual union as its aim. But we do not separate from this—what in any case has a share in the name 'love'—on the one hand, self-love, and on the other, love for parents and children, friendship and love for humanity in general, and also devotion to concrete objects and to abstract ideas. [. . .] In its origin, function, and relation to sexual love, the 'Eros' of the philosopher Plato coincides exactly with the love-force, the libido of psycho-analysis, [. . .] and when the apostle Paul, in his famous epistle to the Corinthians, praises love above all else, he certainly understands it in the same 'wider' sense." (Freud, 1921c, pp. 90–91)

There is no doubt that sexual love, love for one's partner, has its roots in the body and is linked to the instinctual drives, to the libido. Narcissism too is linked as much to the sexual instinct as to the death drive. Freud writes of narcissistic libido directed towards the ego, differentiating it from object-libido directed towards another person (Freud, 1914c). The reader may well be surprised to find, in some psychoanalytic writings,[3] that narcissism and drive-related elements are contrasted.

Love conceived of as Eros is carnal, it is caught up in the metabolism of hormones and shifts in humours, the physical coming-together of bodies. Sometimes the term "platonic love" is used to designate the fact that no carnal element is present; this is essentially a reference to Plato's *Symposium*, in which the philosopher develops the idea of elevation through love of beautiful bodies to love of beauty itself, to the Idea of Beauty, the Idea of Good. Plato himself, however, does not appear to have been particularly platonic in his love of young men ... We could perhaps speak of a mythical Eros, the elevation of man towards God in the Hellenistic mysteries, whereas Christian love descends from God towards man.

Philia

Philia refers to friendship,[4] far removed from the tumultuous passion of Eros, from the uncertainty of reciprocity, from the mixture of sensuality and tenderness. Friendship implies an equality of communication, reciprocity, and pure tenderness with no hint of sensuality. If we follow Freud, since tenderness is one of the two currents of sexuality, sexuality also has its place in friendship. Tenderness is emotion incarnate, but sexual relations do not come into it.

Does this mean that friendship is not present in a two-person relationship as a couple? On the contrary, if the couple are in a lasting relationship, if intimacy is part of their shared experience, this is because, in addition to the sexual urge—which represents an obstacle to overcoming bodily differences in sensitivity and functioning—tenderness is present; tenderness, friendship, Philia.

Friendship is not narcissistic, it focuses on and attempts to understand the other person, and tries not to demand what he or she is not able to give. Saint-Exupéry describes it beautifully in his "Letter to a hostage" (1944; 1986, pp. 118–119):

"I am so tired of polemics, exclusivities, and fanaticisms! I can call on you without putting on any uniform, without having to recite any creed, without having to abdicate any part of my inner self. With you, I do not have to exonerate myself, or plead a cause, or prove a point; I find peace [. . .]. I—who like all others want to be recognized—feel pure in you and am drawn toward you. I am drawn to where I feel pure. It was not my formulas nor my reasoning that taught you what I am. It was the acceptance of what I am that made you indulgent toward my formulas and my reasoning. I am grateful to you for accepting me at my face value. Of what use is a friend who sits in judgement on me? If I invite a friend to join me for a meal and he's limping, I do not ask him to dance but to sit down."

Friendship hopes for reciprocity, it is fuelled by reciprocity. If reciprocity breaks down, suffering is the result. Friendship is elective, selective and implies affinity: "Because it was him, because it was me," said Montaigne. In this sense, the commandment "love thy neighbour . . ."—in other words any unspecified person at all, even one's enemy—is related not to friendship but to another kind of love, *Agapè*.

Agapè

In modern Greek, *Agapè* simply means "love", but in ancient Greek it was "almost unknown to secular vocabulary" (Chouraqui, 1982); it appears in the Greek translation of the Septuagint Bible and in the New Testament. The word was not created by the apostle Paul, but he is the one who introduced it "as a specific denomination designating Christian love" (Nygren, 1930). It is the key word in Chapter 13 of Paul's first Epistle to the Corinthians; an inspired text if ever there was one.

Reading the various translations of the Bible makes it clear that the translator's craft ought deservedly to have been included in Freud's list of impossible professions alongside those of parent, psychoanalyst and government leader - *erziehen, kurieren, regieren*. It is impossible to render the sounds, the alliterations and all the connotations of the original text.

Agapè has been translated from the original Greek into Latin as *caritas*. In German, all the translations I have had occasion to look at use the term *Liebe*. The Authorized Version of the Bible says *charity*. In French, translations alternate between *charité* and *amour*. The Jerusalem Bible, Crampon's Catholic Bible, and Segond's Protestant Bible all say *charité*; the vernacular translation, Chouraqui's translation and the ecumenical translation all use the term *amour*. *Charité* evokes the idea of "giving alms" or other help; but the kind of love referred to here has nothing to do with "good deeds" or "good works". The ecumenical translation of the Bible translates Agapè by *amour* (love) in the body of the chapter, but sub-titles Chapter 13 as "brotherly love", which is regrettable: brotherly love is evocative of the love that brothers can feel for each other—friendship, in other words—whereas here it is a matter of the love that one has for one's neighbour, i.e. the kind of love that is possible only through the love that God has for mankind. It is true, of course, that "agapes" were the communal, brotherly meals of early Christian fellowship—but what a watering-down to talk of brotherly love when the entire text is a "hymn to love": the love of God, the love that man could never succeed in achieving for God or for his fellow men were it not for the love that God has for mankind. Here is the chapter as it appears in the Authorized Version of the Bible (where the term *charity* is used):

Corinthians I, 13:

Though I speak with the tongues of men and of angels, and have not charity, I am become as sounding brass, or a tinkling cymbal.

And though I have the gift of prophecy, and understand all mysteries, and all knowledge; and though I have all faith, so that I could remove mountains, and have not charity, I am nothing.

And though I bestow all my goods to feed the poor, and though I give my body to be burned, and have not charity, it profiteth me nothing.

Charity suffereth long, and is kind; charity envieth not; charity vaunteth not itself, is not puffed up,

Doth not behave itself unseemly, seeketh not her own, is not easily provoked, thinketh no evil;

Rejoiceth not in iniquity, but rejoiceth in the truth;

Beareth all things, believeth all things, hopeth all things, endureth all things.

Charity never faileth: but whether there be prophecies, they shall fail; whether there be tongues, they shall cease; whether there be knowledge, it shall vanish away.

For we know in part, and we prophesy in part.

But when that which is perfect is come, then that which is in part shall be done away.

When I was a child, I spake as a child, I understood as a child, I thought as a child: but when I became a man, I put away childish things.

For now we see through a glass, darkly; but then face to face: now I know in part; but then shall I know even as also I am known.

And now abideth faith, hope, charity, these three; but the greatest of these is charity.

If one does not adopt a Christian point of view, this kind of love is impossible; as I have pointed out, it can come only from God's love for mankind, from divine grace. Point taken.

However, even if we do not adopt the point of view of Christian faith, the text is telling us, over and beyond the unattainable dimension of grace, of an ideal that guides us in certain circumstances. It contrasts deeds, some of great worth, and the inspiration that lies behind them. It tells of an attitude towards other people that is not guided by negativity, of a love disengaged from the ambivalence in which hate and love are entangled. It tells of object-love as contrasted with narcissistic love, of a love in which concern for others is more important that the need to protect oneself. It tells of a love that will not fail. It contrasts infantile with adult (in drawing this contrast, Paul says "child" and "man": as he wrote his epistle, he did not forget that he himself was a man. One may hope, all the same, that he did not intend to exclude women from his overall message.).

I may perhaps shock both Christians and my fellow psychoanalysts: the "benevolent neutrality" of psychoanalysis seems to me to participate in this dimension of Agapè. It is more benevolence than neutrality (if neutrality implies coolness and indifference), and the neutrality it refers to has in fact to do with not being self-centred, not allowing any room for egocentricity. Of course, the psychoanalyst is paid a fee (though at times an analyst may decide not to ask for payment), but within the analytical setting, the attitude of the analyst is very reminiscent of some form of Agapè. It is a matter of not being there in the slightest degree in order to satisfy one's personal desires, or to expect the patient to contribute to one's own gratification; the whole focus is on the attempt to understand the patient in his or her distress and vicissitudes, even though, at times, they may be extremely difficult to bear. If the patient says something unpleasant about the analyst, by not taking offence at this, the latter can try to understand this "negative transference" and to interpret it in more favourable circumstances—i.e. when the patient becomes able to see that these are in fact his or her own projections. The analyst has to "hold on" for as long as it takes. I believe that psychoanalysts are capable of this kind of benevolence. It is regrettable, all the same, that outside of the analytical setting, that capacity seems all too often to disappear. Crossing the frontier is clearly a serious mistake—when an analyst responds to his patient's feelings (this situation almost always involves a male analyst and a female patient) on the level of Eros and not on that of Agapè, i.e. by having sexual intercourse with her.

Every therapeutic attitude, every situation in which one places oneself at someone else's service, involves something to do with Agapè. In every love relationship between human beings, Agapè has a place. Love between human beings, love within a couple, parents' love for their children—Agapè is part of all this. Can we speak of love if the search for sexual satisfaction is all there is, a short-lived passionate relationship, a possessive kind of love? Or even a friendship in which the expectation of reciprocity prevails over understanding, patience and benevolence? Is there any love worthy of the name that does not include something given willingly and without payment to the other person?

Sometimes the term "oblatory love" is used to designate Agapè, but it is a cold, remote and in addition suspect term (the question is, what lies behind oblation?).

Does any pure form of Agapè exist? Perhaps, from a Christian perspective. From the perspective I take here, however, all love involving human beings needs to be embodied physically, subjected to the demands of the human body. Do ascetic mortifications enable Agapè to blossom forth, or are they the buds of narcissistic masochism? Once again, it is as though one were thinking of oneself, not of the other person. Can all erotic needs be sublimated?

How does Buddhistic compassion compare with Agapè? In French, the term *compassion*, often given more or less as a synonym for pity, carries an air of condescension, which is not the case with *karuna*. *Karuna* is "awareness of solidarity in suffering with all beings, and the firm belief that the most effective way of freeing oneself from one's suffering is to work at freeing others from theirs." (Massein, 1997, p. 1022); it is "universal benevolence. In Buddhism, compassion does not connote anything painful or depressing. Nor is it a particular kind of activism. It is a serene and radiating force that is projected on to every being." (Thierry, 1997, p. 1806). The Great Compassion, with no reference to beings or to reality, depends on attaining emptiness, in which the concepts of *me* and *others* have no place. (Rimpochè, in Lenoir & Masquelier, t. II, 1997, p. 1808; Silburn, 1997, *passim*). When he returned to the world after his Illumination, Buddha was full of compassion. Buddhism denounces the misery of the human condition, with its destiny of illness, old age, death, and loss of the person one loves, as well as the re-birth cycle that only the extinction of desire can interrupt. Although there may not be in compassion the great mystical blaze of Agapè, it has to be acknowledged that, in Buddhism, there are no painful myths, no original sin, no sacrifice accomplished in the name of humanity which one is required to share through suffering. Buddha opens the door to suppressing the desire that maintains the cycle of suffering and re-birth, and he smiles. Agapè may be a gift from God, attaining Grace may not depend on us, but benevolence and compassion depend solely on the work we do on and with ourselves in order to control our desires.

Notes

1 Not all psychoanalysts define primary narcissism in the same way.
2 See the present author's *Homo Psychanalyticus* (1990), [in French] in particular the chapters entitled "Re-reading Freud's text on the compulsion to repeat: clinical theory and philosophical speculation" and "Compulsion to repeat and death instinct".
3 In those of Bela Grunberger, for example.
4 It should be observed that, when the idea of friendship is highly praised, it is almost always friendship between men that is being referred to, not that between women. Friendship between a man and a woman is generally thought to be impossible ...

CHAPTER EIGHT

Sex makes the world go round

At every moment in life, each of us is either a man or a woman. We go beyond this division into two sexes only at the highest level of thinking, of reflection, of abstract thought.

At the same time, the question of how we position ourselves with respect to others is constantly present, hence the challenge not only to our identity as such but also to our chances of being loved. Those who belong to the opposite sex are in a quite specific position in this respect.

Advertising our gender

At every moment in life, each of us is either a man or a woman. Is it right or wrong that everything should remind us of this? Our first (given) name, the clothes we wear, the tasks we undertake, our status in society? Ought we to emphasize these sex characteristics or attenuate them? Is it easier to obtain equality when the sex to which we belong is ignored or, on the contrary, emphasized? Every society reminds its members of the existence of the sexual difference, but in an arbitrary manner, by imposing attitudes and ways of doing things. Although we cannot erase that difference, we can fight against arbitrariness in the way society interprets it whenever this leads to deprivation of rights or of personal liberty.

The initial constraint is represented by our *first name*, the one that is assigned to us at birth. In most cases, our given names clearly indicate our gender. In French, there are a few ambi-gender or androgynous first names, sometimes described as ambivalent: Camille, Claude, Dominique; more numerous are those that are pronounced in the same way but spelled differently: Daniel/Danièle or Danielle, Michel/Michèle or Michelle, René/Renée, André/ Andrée, etc. In everyday life we can use some other name (another first name, or a diminutive), take what is called a customary name that will be inscribed on our identity card after our legal name—but we cannot change our registered first name (and a fortiori our surname) without due legal process. Transsexuals know this problem well. Those who do have an ambi-gender first name are happy to show identity papers that enable them to go unnoticed at a time when they are changing sex; often others who have entered a request for permission to change their first name—this is granted more easily than a change in civil status—are authorized to do so on condition that they choose an ambi-gender name only. Any indication added to their given name (sex, profession if "genderized" by noun feminization) aggravates their situation. Some jurists have suggested that one's identity papers should no longer carry any mention of sex at all . . . (Council of Europe, 1995).

In foreign languages, first names can sometimes be misleading. When one quotes an author, one is supposed to be able to identify him or her correctly. Unfortunately, often very little is known about the gender of first names in languages other than one's own. I have myself blundered at times. In the first book I wrote (*L'Enfant de Six Ans et Son Avenir*), I quoted extensively Eve Malmquist, convinced that I was talking about a woman writer; in Swedish, however, Eve is a male first name, not a female one—the female first name corresponding to Ève in French (or to Eve in English) is Eva. Similarly, I realized that Lee N. Robins, (whom I quoted extensively in the same book), was a woman when I met her in person: she laughed at my mistake. Lee is an ambi-gender first name in English. I thought I could avoid such mishaps by referring in the body of my text simply to "the author";[1] this, however, would not be the case were we to adopt the accepted usage in Quebec and in French-speaking Switzerland, where they distinguish between *auteur* (masculine) and *auteure* (feminine).

Linguistic usage in French makes *gender agreement* obligatory. There is a militant movement which demands that nouns relating to professions be feminized where necessary; but far from reducing the importance of gender, this would actually reinforce it. No-one yet seems to have come to the conclusion that gender agreement in grammar should be abolished altogether (in English, for example, it applies to all intents and purposes only to personal and possessive pronouns and adjectives of possession). We are victims of an Indo-European illusion: because Indo-European languages recognize two (masculine and feminine) or three (masculine, feminine and neuter) genders, we imagine that no language could do without this kind of system. In fact, most languages (for example, Chinese) do not make any gender distinctions at all (Corbett, 1991); in other words, they do not have a system of grammatical agreement based on the category "gender". Other languages have multiple systems of agreement based on various categories (some as many as twenty). But no society does without gender role differentiation. Gender is not attributed exclusively in accordance with meaning (i.e. sex) but follows also certain rules linked to the morphology of the word involved (for example, in German, *Fraulein*, Miss, is neuter because all words ending in *-lein* are neuter); the masculine gender is not always the dominant one when it comes to attributing gender or rules governing plural agreement when nouns are of different genders (in French, in this case, agreement always takes the masculine form).

What advantages are women really gaining thanks to feminization of nouns relating to professions? Of course the question does not raise the same issues in English, where grammatical gender plays only a limited role, as it does in French, where this role is crucial. What have I gained now that I am deemed to be *une auteure, une écrivaine, une professeure, une docteure* rather than *un auteur, un écrivain, un professeur, un docteur*? Many feminists do see this as an objective to be fought for; I am thinking, for example, of Benoîte Groult's *Histoire d'une Éva-sion* (1997). What seems to me important is that I have written books, taught, practised psychiatry (and I am delighted to remain '*psychiatre*' and '*psychanalyste*' without any need for "genderization").[2] Perhaps Benoîte Groult feels that the feminization of such nouns is important because for many a long year she was treated as an inferior because she was a woman and it was only fairly recently that she woke up to the fact that she had the right to exist differently. Perhaps I do not feel the feminization of nouns relating to professions to be a particularly important issue because I was brought up without ever having had it said to me, even by implication, that, because I was a girl, some doors would remain closed to me; it went without saying that I was to "study" and do my schoolwork properly, find a job, sit my driving test as soon as I turned 18, etc. In my career I have never encountered any obstacles relating to the fact that I am a woman: it is true that I became a university professor in psychology—in medicine, it would have been quite a different matter. Yet I have found myself rebelling in a feminist way as regards the status of women, and I expressed this in the very first paper I published: I observed that women were doing the cooking every day (something I like doing, by the way) yet no-one could ever imagine a great chef being a woman. Inventing the word *cheffe* will not change this situation; change will come about thanks to the fact that some women—still very few in number—have managed to impose themselves as chefs (or cheffes); and even then what they do is called "women's cuisine" . . . Feminization of nouns relating to professions is something that comes as an aftermath to symbolize the progress that has been accomplished—but at the same time it reinforces the "gender bias" in everything we do; women henceforth have to announce their profession in a grammatically-accepted way, at least in a language like French, in which grammatical gender plays an important role; in English, where gender is reduced to its simplest form, the feminist combat will not have to manifest its gains in that manner. It is not by changing words that we change situations, it is because situations have changed that we think it might be appropriate to change the words used to refer to them. I would like to be convinced that any man who agitates for the feminization of such nouns has elsewhere in his life done everything he could to advance the cause of women, so that his wife may have the right to the same kind of professional existence as he himself has.

Conversely, the prohibition against sex discrimination in "situations vacant" adverts leads to such picturesque announcements as the following (seen in Australia): "Wanted: barman or barmaid able to wear a mini-skirt".

Social stereotypes govern the way in which we have to *dress*, although nowadays fashion is to some extent unisex as well as being less restrictive.

In everyday life, women are perhaps still treated as sex objects in the way that has so often been denounced. By dressing in such a way as to excite men sexually, women in fact behave, willingly or otherwise, as if they were indeed sex objects. Clinical experience shows that it is not the women who have the most "sophisticated" appearance who are the "hottest" of lovers.

No woman is obliged to wear a mini-skirt (see above) or to go about *topless* unless she wants a job in a particular kind of bar. Women dress the way they want, and often wear jeans or trousers, even if children in their manifest declarations about the difference between the sexes resort to hackneyed stereotypes such as: "girls have long hair and wear skirts"—this is easier to say than: "girls don't have the same kind of widdler", because it avoids having to implicate one's body and to cope with the questions or even anxieties linked to it. Children take social stereotypes as a basis for reinforcing their gender identity, even when they are raised by feminist parents: for example, a girl whose mother never wears anything other than trousers asks her mother to wear a skirt from time to time and make herself "beautiful" . . .

In our civilization, women have full access to *education*, a condition sine qua non for access to equality of rights and personal liberty (Afghan fundamentalists recognized this a contrario when they prohibited girls from attending school). In France, women follow the same curriculum as men. They practice sport; but they do come up against the limitations of nature when they compete against boys. What is more important: competitiveness, with its insane attempts to go further and further, and the pathology into which we force top-level athletes? Or the simple fact of being able to swim, ride a bicycle, practice judo or karate whenever we want?

The *manner* in which we behave and conduct ourselves is also decided by cultural tradition. Here too, in our society, we have evolved towards leaving more freedom to the individual. However, although boyish behaviour is accepted in girls, girlish behaviour in boys is definitely frowned upon. A girl can wear jeans and climb trees; but a boy cannot wear a skirt, simper, enjoy knitting . . . It is obvious that society wants the difference between the sexes to be clearly advertised, and also that there is a rejection of femininity. Once again we encounter the notion of treating women as inferior, together with the fear of passivity (Schaeffer, 1997).

Differences in *status* and issues of parity are very much on the agenda today, especially as regards politics and political careers. Soon women will no longer have inferior status in this domain. Nobody nowadays would dare say that women ought to busy themselves with their cooking-pots and not with running the affairs of the *polis*.

Depending on whether we see the bottle as half-full or as half-empty, we either denounce *male domination*[3] (and we are right to denounce it) or talk of the feminist revolution (and much progress has indeed been accomplished). In my view, the condition of women has radically and irreversibly changed in our culture since the end of the Second World War.

Nature and culture

If the quest for equality of status does not seem to me to stand in opposition to the sexual difference, there are other objectives that in one way or another aim to deny that difference and try to abolish it.

Arguments such as "it's against nature" or "it's natural" are poor arguments. It is in the nature of man to have culture, and culture is a transformation of nature. The question is how far can we go in transforming nature without de-naturing it, without destroying rather than improving it? Can human beings be "masters and possessors of nature" without paying due heed to nature itself?

The argument that consists in accepting only natural methods of contraception is a misleading one. What we now know of a woman's periodic cycle, of rectal temperature or the state of her mucus during the cycle, derives not from natural instinct but from scientific and technical investigation acquired through animal manipulation and experimentation.

The argument according to which homosexuality is against nature does not hold water either. Homosexuality occurs in animals and, in one form or another, is found in all human societies. It is not, however, the exclusive or preferred form of sexual gratification in any animal species or in any human society; were this the case, it would lead to the extinction of that species or to the disappearance of that society.

But what are we doing when we "change sex", or try to make it possible for a man to bear a child in his peritoneum?

Every society has to confront the sexual difference. Society of course interprets that difference when it defines masculine and feminine, and imposes certain constraints that may not go unchallenged.

But we could say too that society symbolizes it, and makes it negotiable and constructive. Acknowledging that the sexes and procreation exist, that the differences between the sexes and between generations exist also, is just as fundamental for the sociologist or anthropologist as it is for the psychoanalyst. These differences organize kinship relations and remind us that we are part of a line of descent (in a cognate system such as ours, of *two* lines of descent), and that spontaneous generation does not exist.

Laws are not natural, they are culturally-determined. The laws that govern kinship relations can be changed—as indeed they have been, which is why it is impossible to speak of *the Law*, as is sometimes done with reference to the prohibition against incest. There is no universal definition of incest, but there is also no example of a society in which no unions are prohibited; this, according to Lévi-Strauss, is the negative side of the positive possibility for everyone to take a spouse or partner.

One of the issues on the agenda concerns whether or not it is acceptable for a child to be the son or daughter of two fathers (and no mother) or of two mothers (and no father). Irène Théry (1997, 1998), who interviewed many same-sex couples in the context of an investigation into AIDS, is in favour of everything that enables each partner to be supportive of the other in such couples; but she feels that endorsing access by same-sex couples to parenthood would undermine the symbolic foundations of society. As a child psychiatrist and psychoanalyst, I look at the situation from a different perspective.

Sufficient time has not yet elapsed for us to have reliable studies of the long-term impact of such situations. At present we find ourselves having to deal with an entirely new situation, the outcome of which depends very much on how mentalities evolve. Increased tolerance of such arrangements is necessary if children are not to suffer from social stigmata—we cannot and must not count exclusively on their own resilience. In his *Métamorphoses de la parenté* (2004, p. 577–587), Godelier has some very pertinent remarks to make about the novelty of this situation from an anthropological point of view; he highlights the danger of what he calls "heterophobia"—a kind of "whiplash hate" that is in itself comprehensible "coming from people who, for decades, have suffered social, physical and symbolic violence because of their sexual orientation".

The torments of sexuality

If instinct in human beings could dictate their conduct in an inflexible, precise and inevitable manner, they would not be as tormented by sexuality as they are. There is no pre-inscribed norm in their make-up, yet the need for norms renders them vulnerable to the dictates of the *socius*. Conflict arises between a pleasurable experience and the idea that perhaps that pleasure is not legitimate, or is less intense than what other people experience, (imagined as magnificent and without defect).

Children, adolescents and adults decipher what they feel, what they experience in their body, with the help of the keys provided by the *socius*. There is what is officially transmitted by cultural tradition via its foundation codes of law, religious dogma and literature. There is what comes from the parents, what they say and how they behave, their fantasies and affects communicated without their realizing it. There is what comes from the peer-group, in which the story of what was really experienced is mingled with fantasies concerning it.

What our cultural tradition transmits ought really to be called *the lie told by culture*.

Prohibitions are transmitted—but nobody follows them to the letter; at times, transgression meets with approval, at others it is disapproved of and persecuted. That spouses be faithful to each other is prescribed, because marriage is a sacrament in Roman Catholicism; yet the sexual escapades of the Kings of France, Catholic to a man, are well known, and their illegitimate children were raised with their offspring born in wedlock; the tumultuous love life of Henry VIII, with its occasionally murderous outcome, was partly the reason for the founding of the Church of England. Celibacy is imposed on priests, but this was not always the case—for example, during the first millennium. The pope is supposed not to have a sexual or marital life, yet by means of encyclicals he governs the sexual and marital life of the faithful, who obey or not as the case may be. Morality is discredited by hypocrisy, and at the same time individuals feel the need to find values other than the traditional ones linked to religion or social class, in order to solve the new problems resulting from advances in science and technology; that is why we often prefer to speak of "ethics" rather than of "morality"—ethics are thought of as being the product of one's own thinking.

Masturbation met with strong religious disapproval; this did not perhaps create masturbatory guilt feelings, but it certainly reinforced them. If it is easy for religion to make people feel guilty, this is because individuals feel anxious about what occurs without their willing it and without their being able to control it. Masturbation was also the object of medical condemnation, leading to the "great fear" of the 19th Century (Stengers & van Neck, 1984). Masturbation was said to make people go mad or become idiots, it led to all sorts of diseases, etc. Freud himself—although he is considered as being the moving force behind a healthier perspective on masturbation—approved little Hans's mother when she admonished her son for masturbating; Freud says that she "had a predestined part to play" (1909b, p. 28). Nowadays, we would look upon masturbation as giving cause for concern only if it were compulsive and public; we are more worried by someone who maintains that he or she has never masturbated. Masturbation exists in animals and in every human society (Ford & Beach, 1951).

What is the nature of sexual pleasure? How do we know what our partner is feeling, apart from what he or she tells us? It is difficult enough to imagine what someone of the same sex feels, even though the fact of belonging to the same sex is a facilitating and reassuring factor in homosexuality; how can we imagine what someone of the opposite sex feels, when we cannot have recourse to our own bodily experience as such, when we have only a possibility of empathy—and then only if we are not afraid of identifying with our partner?

This issue is so important that many patients declare that they are dissatisfied with their sex life, even though what they go on to describe would seem to indicate that quite a lot of people would be perfectly happy to have what they experience. What are the norms of reference, when we learn that, before the last war, a man in the United States was convicted of perversion because he asked his wife to have intercourse three times per week? One of my patients described the vaginal orgasm she had had—while refusing to recognize it as a vaginal orgasm because the feminist group to which she belonged had declared that vaginal orgasms did not exist and were merely something that men had invented to keep women in a subordinate role.

In order to be satisfied with what one feels, there has to be a whole process of learning to trust oneself, a process of self-esteem and self-assertiveness. In groups that practice "new therapies", participants are taught that they will have made good progress once they are able to say to people who ask them what they felt: "I felt exactly what I should feel".

If, independently of the comparisons we make with other people, what we feel does not seem to be satisfactory, we find ourselves on the brink of a complicated form of suffering: either our partner stands accused of not doing what was required, or else in a depressive movement we accuse ourselves of not being capable of attaining sexual climax. The fact that in heterosexual intercourse the time frame and the modalities necessary for reaching a climax differ as between men and women does not help matters.

As far as the lie of culture is concerned, literature is something a special case. Romantic literature springs not only from an author's imagination, experience (naturally enough) and observations, but also from his or her dreams, with their voluntary or involuntary distortions, defensive in nature. If we read books, literature is at the very heart of our sentimental education. And even if culture lies, it is better to read than to be left with nothing but silly chitter-chatter; it is better to put one's imagination to work than to be traversed by an impulse to act.

Literature lies. We do not go into a swoon at the press of a button like heroines in some novels do, as a means of escaping from some inconvenient situation—we have to drink the cup of disappointment down to the last dregs. It is true of course that literature can offer us beautiful myths—but we have to be clear about the meaning of myth.

Don Juan is wonderful, especially with Mozart's music in our ears. Who does not love Don Juan, with his irresistible sparkle? But when we find ourselves the victim of a man who goes from seduction to seduction, a man whose only thought is to add your name to his *catalogo*, then he is no more than a boor, an ordinarily cruel man who defends himself against his fear of love and of intimacy by lying and running away.

As I said before, men are polygamous—but not simply polygamous, in the sense that they need several unions. They need also to seduce and to verify constantly that their seductive powers have not diminished—as if it were the equivalent of verifying the integrity of their body and their mind.

A woman desperately needs to be loved, to live in the security of love, nestling into a man's bosom (men have bosoms too), protected from what she feels as her weakness, rewarded for what she feels is her daily dedication and her gift of what lies deep inside her. For women more than for men, making a success of life depends on having a successful love life. That may be one of the obstacles women encounter with respect to professional success.

Love can be happy—a couple can be happy—only if they go on making adjustments and concessions, which should not be experienced as so many sacrifices. In other words, there are so few happy couples . . . but there are some, all the same. The fact that very little is said about them is worth thinking about. Why do artistic productions have a preference for showing us the harmful and unhappy side of things? In order to exorcize suffering? Because happiness cannot be attained through impregnation of the imagination? Happiness is not spectacular, it is internal, private, and radiates outwards only towards those who are attentive to others.

Forgetting sex

I have insisted on the fact that, at every moment in life, each of us is either a man or a woman; this does not mean that humanity is divided into two halves. Humanity is both man and woman. It can come to fruition in each of us only if we are capable of empathizing with what the other person of the opposite sex is feeling; if we are capable of identifying with that person without fear and without envy. Envy can be dispelled, contrary to what Freud said of penis envy. Neither of the sexes or genders is favoured more than the other, they are simply two ways of living the human condition through a process that is, moreover, a highly personal itinerary; of that it is possible to become aware. The life of the other person looks better only when seen from the outside; we project on to him or her the idea of some invulnerable strength while feeling ourselves to be so fragile. Humanity comes to fruition inside us only through psychic bisexuality, the capacity to experience within ourselves, through identification, both masculine and feminine dimensions in their very being—masculine desire and feminine desire. Christian David has emphasized the role of "bisexual mediation" (1975).

Sex and gender are not implicated in every one of our thinking processes. The more purely cognitive they are, the more asexual or desexualized. I know that people who have studied brain functioning have attempted to discover differences in activated zones, particularly as regards the use of the hemispheres, in men and in women; as I have pointed out, these are not all-or-nothing differences. But above all, the result of these thinking processes is the same: two plus two makes four. I would even argue that the aim of thinking is to be desexualized. Scientific and cultural productions are the outcome of sublimation, in other words of what Freud described as drives inhibited as to their sexual aim. Desexualization is less obvious when it comes to the sex of the emotions (Braconnier, 1996), dominated by the system of hormones and humours.

Though desire may be permanent on a latent level, it explodes consciously only from time to time. There are so many things to keep us busy, some of which are necessary for survival (work, preparing food, etc.), others are sublimated and give us pleasure, joy, and happiness. Human beings are not mayflies; we do not die as soon as we have mated. Those who have not produced children may well have made other contributions to the social sphere: Maurice Godelier emphasizes the fact that it is not the species but social relationships which human beings perpetuate. Animals perpetuate their species, man is a product of culture, never purely of biology. This could lead us to exalt the capacities of human beings; it is also the source of all sorts of particularisms, of the "narcissism of minor differences" as Freud put it (1918 [1917], p. 199), of all the racist ideologies in the name of which men kill one another.

Sexual desire haunts us constantly but softly, the drives exert permanent pressure, wrote Freud. He spoke also of *Miterregung*, a term that appears under various guises in the *Standard Edition*: sympathetic excitement, libidinal sympathetic excitation, excitation, accompanying excitation, accompanying sexual excitation, and concomitant sexual excitation. It would have been better to translate the term systematically as "co-excitation": the idea is that some sexual arousal always accompanies powerful excitation, whatever its nature. Freud uses the term only nine times in all of his writings, yet it is a notion that has proved extremely important for some French psychoanalysts (Braunschweig & Fain, 1971; Parat, 1995).

Sex is the primary driving force of all, and is at the origin of the birth of a new human being; we like to think of ourselves as the fruit of a loving relationship between two human beings rather than as an encounter between two cells. Medically-assisted procreation can suppress intercourse and reduce the actual sexual part to an encounter between two sex cells—and cloning can do away even with that . . .

Sex is not everything, but sex makes the world go round. In the various *oeuvres* that culture offers, sex only *appears* to be forgotten. Sexual desire channels our energy into aims that are not in themselves sexual. Faced with Thanatos (the forces of destruction), we place all our hopes in Eros, Philia and Agapè; and so we find ourselves at one with Freud as he wrote the closing sentences of *Civilization and its Discontents*—before the Second World War, the concentration camps, the atomic bomb: "And now it is to be expected that the other of the two 'Heavenly Powers', eternal Eros, will make an effort to assert himself in the struggle with his equally immortal adversary." (1930a, pp. 14–54)

Notes

1   "L'auteur" being a masculine-gender word in French, all grammatical agreements (adjectives, pronouns, etc.) would be masculine, whatever the actual sex of the author. (Translator's note)

2   Whether one is a male or female psychiatrist or psychoanalyst, the spelling of the noun in French is the same: (*un* or *une*) *psychiatre*, (*un* or *une*) *psychanalyste*. (Translator's note)

3   The original French version of this book was completed when Pierre Bourdieu's book *Male Domination* (1998) was published. His conclusions are complex: "Divulging the scientific analysis of a form of domination necessarily has an impact on the *socius*, though this can lie in one of two opposite directions: either it will symbolically reinforce the domination [. . .] or contribute to neutralizing it." (op. cit., p. 121). For Bourdieu, "the tremendous work of criticism carried out by the feminist movement" has contributed to change; his analysis of the factors that bring about such changes to some extent matches my own, in particular as regards the role of formal education, though his standpoint is that of a sociologist (op. cit. p. 95 et seq.).

References

Abensour, L. (1921). *Histoire générale du féminisme: Des origines à nos jours.* Paris-Genève réédition: Slatkine Reprints, 1979.

Adler, L. (1990). *La vie quotidienne dans les maisons closes 1830–1930.* Paris: Hachette.

Andreas-Salomé, L. (1916). Anal and Sexual [Anal wnd Sexal]. *Imago,* 6, 429–273.

Alain (1934). Les dieux, *Les arts et les dieux.* Paris: Gallimard, La Pléiade, 1958.

Arnaud-Duc, N. (1991). Les contradictions du droit. In: G. Duby & M. Perrot (Eds.), *Histoire des femmes,* Vol. 4, 87–116.

Balier, C. (1988). *Psychanalyse des comportements violents.* Paris: PUF.

Balier, C. (1996). *Psychanalyse des comportements sexuels violents: Une pathologie de l'inachèvement,* Paris: PUF.

Balier, C., (Ed.),(1997). with Ciavaldini, A. & Girard-Khayat, M. *Rapport de recherche sur les agresseurs sexuels.* Paris: Direction générale de la santé.

Barry, K. (1995). *The Prostitution of Sexuality.* New York: New York University Press.

Baudelot, C., & Establet R. (1992), *Allez les filles!,* Paris: Seuil.

Beauvoir, S. de (1949). *Le Deuxième Sexe.* Paris: Gallimard. *The Second Sex.* Translated and edited by H.M.Parshley, with an introduction by M. Crosland. New York: Alfred A. Knopf, 1993.

Belaïsch, J., & Kervasdoué, A. de (1996). *Questions d'hommes.* Paris: Odile Jacob.

Ben Jelloun, T. (1985). *L'enfant de sable,* Paris: Seuil. *The Sand Child.* Translated by A. Sheridan. Harcourt, 1987.

Ben Jelloun, T. (1987). *La nuit sacrée.* Paris: Seuil. *The Sacred Night.* Translated by A. Sheridan. Harcourt, 1989.

Bichet, X. (1800). *Recherches physiologiques sur la vie et la mort*. Paris: Flammarion, 1994.

Bourdieu, P. (1998). *La domination masculine*, Paris: Seuil.

Bowlby, J. (1969–1980), *Attachment and Loss*. The Tavistock Institute of Human Relations. Vol. 1, *Attachment*, New York: Basic Books, 1969. Vol. 2, *Separation: Anxiety and Anger*. New York: Basic Books, 1973. Vol. 3, *Loss: Sadness and Depression*. London: The Hogarth Press, 1980.

Braconnier, A. (1996). *Le sexe des émotions*. Paris: Odile Jacob.

Bradley, Susan J., Oliver, Gillian D., Chernik Avinoam, B., & Zucker, Kenneth J. (1998). Experiment of nurture: ablatio penis at 2 months, sex reassignment at 7 months, and a psychosexual follow-up in young adulthood. *Pediatrics, 102,* 1, July, 5 pages. E91-E95.

Braunschweig, D., & Fain M. (1971). *Eros et Anteros*. Paris: PUF.

Brisson, L. (1997). *Le sexe incertain: Androgynes, hermaphrodites et métamorphoses dans l'Antiquité,* Paris: Les Belles Lettres.

Bullough, V., with the assistance of Bullough, B. (1973). *The Subordinate Sex: A History of Attitudes towards Women*. Urbana, Ill.: University of Illinois Press.

Bullough, V. L. (1979). *Homosexuality: A History, From Ancient Greece to Gay Liberation*, New York: Meridian.

Carl, D. (1990). *Counselling Same-Sex Couples*. New York: W. W. Norton.

Chasseguet-Smirgel, J. (1984). *Ethique et esthétique de la perversion*. Seyssel: éditions du Champ Vallon.

Chasseguet-Smirgel, J. (2003). *Le corps comme miroir du monde*. Paris: PUF.

Chiland, C. (1971). *L'enfant de six ans et son avenir*. Paris: PUF.

Chiland, C. (1990). Freud et e'hériédite *Homo psychanalyticus*. Paris: PUF 121–129.

Chiland, C. (1997). *Changer de sexe*. Paris: Odile Jacob.

Chiland, C. (2003a). *Robert Jesse Stoller*. Paris: PUF

Chiland, C. (2003b). *Transsexualism: Illusion and Reality*. trans. P.Slotkin. London & New York: Continuum.

Chiland, C. (2005). *Exploring Transsexualism*, trans. D. Alcorn. London: Karnac.

Chouraqui, A. (1982). *L'Univers de la Bible*. Paris: Éditions Lidis.

Cohn-Bendit, D. (1998). *Une envie de politique*. Entretiens avec Lucas Delattre et Guy Herlich. Paris: La Découverte/Le Monde.

Colapinto, J. (2000). *As Nature Made Him*. London: Quartet Books.

Comte-Sponville, A., & Ferry, L. (1998). *La Sagesse des Modernes: Dix questions pour notre temps*. Paris: Robert Laffont.

Council of Europe (1995). *Transsexualism, Medicine and Law*. 23rd Colloquy on European Law, the Free University of Amsterdam, Netherlands, (14–16th April), 1993. Strasbourg: Editions du Conseil de l'Europe.

Corbett, G. (1991). *Gender*. Cambridge, UK: Cambridge University Press.

Corbin, A. (1978). *Les filles de noce*. Paris: Aubier-Montaigne. Poche. Paris: Flammarion, 1982.

Cramer, E., & McFarlane, J. (1994). Pornography and abuse of women. *Public Health Nursing, 11*: 4, 268–272.

David, C. (1975). La bisexualité psychique: Eléments d'une réévaluation. *Revue française de psychanalyse, 39*: 5–6, 495–856.

Delcourt, M. (1958). *Hermaphrodite. Mythes et rites de la bisexualité dans l'Antiquité classique*. Paris: PUF. Réédition revue, 1992, Collection Dito, p. 137. *Hermaphrodite: Myths and Rites of the Bisexual Figure in Classical Antiquity*. Translated from the French by Jennifer Nicholson. London: Studio Books, 1961.

Deleuze, G. (1967). *Présentation de Sacher-Masoch*, avec le texte intégral de *La Vénus à la fourrure*, traduit de l'allemand par Aude Willm, Paris: Les éditions de Minuit. *Sacher-Masoch: An Interpretation*. Translated from the French by Jean McNeil. London: Faber, 1971.

Deutsch, H. (1945). *The Psychology of Women: A Psychoanalytic Interpretation* (7th ed.), New York: Grune and Stratton.

Diamond M. (1965). A critical evaluation of human sexual behavior. *The Quarterly Review of Biology, 40*, 147–173.

Diamond, M., & Dannemiller, J. E. (1989). Pornography and community standards in Hawaii: Comparison with other states. *Archives of Sexual Behavior, 18*: 6, 475–495.

DSM-IV: Diagnostic and Statistical Manual of Mental Disorders (4th ed.) (1994). Washington D.C.: American Psychiatric Association.

Duby, G., & Perrot, M. (Eds.) (1991). *Histoire des femmes* (5 Vols.) Paris: Plon. *A History of Women in the West*. Cambrige, Mass.: Bellknap Press of Harvard University Press, 1992–1994.

Dumas D. (1990), *La sexualité masculine*. Paris: Albin Michel.

Durkheim, E. (1897). La prohibition de l'inceste et ses origines. *L'Année Sociologique, 1*: 1, 1–70. *Incest; the Nature and Origin of the Taboo*. Translated by Edward Sagarin, together with *The Origins and the Development of the Incest Taboo*, by Albert Ellis, New York: L. Stuart, 1963.

Evans-Pritchard, E. E. (1965). *The Position of Women in Primitive Societies and Other Essays in Social Anthropology*. London: Faber and Faber.

Evans-Pritchard, E. E. (1990). Sexual inversion among the Azande. *American Anthropologist, 72*: 6, (December 1990), 1428–1334.

Fine, A., Le Guen, A., & Oppenheimer, A., (Eds.). (1993). *Les troubles de la sexualité*. Monographies de la Revue Française de Psychanalyse, Paris: PUF.

Ford, C. S., & Beach, F. A. (1951). *Patterns of Sexual Behavior*. New York: Harper and Row.

Foucault, M., *Histoire de la sexualité*, Vol. I, *La volonté de savoir*. Paris, Gallimard, 1976; Vol. II, *L'usage des plaisirs*. Paris: Gallimard, 1984; Vol. III, *Le souci de soi*. Paris, Gallimard, 1984. *The history of sexuality*. Translated from the French by R. Hurley. New York: Vintage Books, 1985.

Foucault, M. présenté par (1978). *Herculine Barbin dite Alexina B.*, Paris: Gallimard. *Herculine Harbin: Being the Recently Discovered Memoirs of a Nineteenth-Century French Hermaphrodite*, introduced by Michel Foucault. Translated by R. McDougall. New York: Pantheon Books, 1980.

Freud, A., & Dann, S. (1951). An experiment in group upbringing. *The Psychoanalytic Study of the Child, 6*: 127–168.

Freud, S. (1895d). *Studies on Hysteria. Standard Edition, 2.*

Freud, S. (1900a). *The Interpretation of Dreams. S.E., 4–5.*

Freud, S. (1905d). *Three Essays on the Theory of Sexuality. S.E., 7.*

Freud, S. (1908d). 'Civilized' sexual morality and modern nervous illness. *S.E., 9,* 179–204.

Freud, S. (1909b). Analysis of a phobia in a five-year old boy. *S.E., 14,* 3–143.

Freud, S. (1910a). Five lectures on psycho-analysis. *S.E., 11,* 3–55.

Freud, S. (1910h). Contribution to the psychology of love, I. A special type of object-choice made by men. *S.E., 11,* 165–175.

Freud, S. (1912d). Contribution to the psychology of love, II. On the universal tendency to debasement in the sphere of love. *S.E., 11,* 179–190.

Freud, S. (1914c). On narcissism: An introduction. *S.E., 14,* 67–102

Freud, S. (1916–1917 [1915–1917]). *Introductory Lectures on Psycho-Analysis. S.E., 15–16.*

Freud, S. (1918 [1917]). The taboo of virginity, *S.E., 11,* 193–208.

Freud, S. (1919e). A child is being beaten. *S.E., 17,* 177–204.

Freud, S. (1920g). *Beyond the Pleasure Principle. S.E., 18,* 3–64.

Freud, S. (1921c). *Group Psychology and the Analysis of the Ego. S.E., 18,* 69–91

Freud, S. (1924c). The economic problem of masochism. *S.E., 19,* 155–170.

Freud, S. (1930a). *Civilization and its Discontents. S.E., 21,* 14–54.

Freud, S. (1940a). *An Outline of Psycho-Analysis. S.E., 23,* 141–207.

Fridell, S. R., Zucker, K. J., Bradley, S. J., & Maing, D. M. (1996). Physical attractiveness of girls with gender identity disorder. *Archives of Sexual Behavior, 25,* 1, 17–31.

Fukui, A., & Westmore, B. (1994). To see or not to see: the debate over pornography and its relationship to sexual aggression. *Australian and New Zealand Journal of Psychiatry, 28,* 4, 600–606.

Godelier, M. (1982). *La production des Grands Hommes: Pouvoir et domination masculine chez les Baruya de Nouvelle-Guinée.* Paris: Fayard. *The Making of Great Men: Male Domination and Power Among the New Guinea Baruya.* Translated by Rupert Swyer. Cambridge, New York: Cambridge University Press; & Paris: Editions de la Maison des Sciences de l'Homme, 1986.

Godelier, M., & Hassoun, J. (1996). *Meurtre du père, sacrifice de la sexualité: Approches anthropologiques et psychanalytiques.* Strasbourg et Paris: Arcanes.

Godelier, M. (2004). *Métamorphoses de la parenté.* Paris: Fayard.

Green, A. (1997). *Les chaînes d'Éros.* Paris: Odile Jacob. *The Chains of Eros: the Sexual in Psychoanalysis.* Translated by L. Thurston. London: Rebus Press, 2000.

Green, R. (2002). Sexual Identity and Sexual Orientation. *Hormones, Brain and Behavior,* Vol. 4, USA: Elsevier Science, 463–485.

Greenson, R. R. (1968). Dis-identifying from mother: its special importance for the boy. *International Journal of Psycho-Analysis, 49,* 370–374.

Grimal, P. (1951). *Dictionnaire de la mythologie grecque et romaine (4th ed.)* Paris: PUF, 1969.

Groult, B. avec l'intervention de Savigneau, J. (1997). *Histoire d'une évasion.* Paris: Grasset.

Habib, C. (1994). *Pensées sur la prostitution.* Paris: Belin.

Halley, J. E. (1989). The politics of the closet: towards equal protection for gay, lesbian, and bisexual identity. *UCLA Law Review, 36,* 5, 915–976.

Halley J. E. (1994), Sexual orientation and the politics of biology: A critique of the argument from immutability. *Stanford Law Review, 46,* 3, (Feb. 1994) 503–568.

Hamer, D., & Copeland, P. (1994). *The Science of Desire: The Search for the Gay Gene and the Biology of Behavior.* New York: Simon & Schuster.

Harlow, H. (1971). *Learning to Love.* New York: Ballantine Books, 1973.

Harvard Law Review (1990). *Sexual Orientation and the Law.* Cambridge, Massachusetts, and London, England: Harvard University Press.

Herdt, G. (1987). *The Sambia: Ritual and Gender in New Guinea.* New York: Holt, Rinehart and Winston.

Héritier, F. (1994). *Les deux sœurs et leur mère: Anthropologie de l'inceste.* Paris: Odile Jacob. *Two Sisters and Their Mother: The Anthropology of Incest.* Translated by J. Herman. New York: Zone Books, London: MIT Press distributor, 1999.

Héritier, F., Cyrulnik, B., Naouri, A., Vrignaud, D., & Xanthakou, M. (1994). *De l'inceste*. Paris: Odile Jacob.

Héritier, F. (1996). *Masculin/Féminin: La pensée de la différence*. Paris: Odile Jacob.

Hermann, K., & Rieck, H. (1978). *Christiane F., Wir Kinder vom Bahnhof Zoo*. Hamburg: Stern-Magazin im Verlag Gruner + Jahr AG & Co., 1978. *Moi, Christiane F., 13 ans, droguée, prostituée . . .* Foreword by H-E. Richter. Translated into French by L. Marcou. Paris: Mercure de France, 1981, Folio, 1982.

Héroard, J. *L'enfant (with a commentary by M. David pp. 321–330) Nouvelle Revue de Psychoanalyse*, 19 (Spring 1979), 281–320

Heusch, L. de (1990). Les vicissitudes de la notion d'interdit. In: J-D.de Lannoy & P. Feyereisen (Eds.), *L'inceste, un siècle d'interpétations*. Paris et Lausanne: Delachaux et Niestlé, 1996.

Howit, D. (1995). Pornography and the paedophile: is it criminogenic? *British Journal of Medical Psychology, 68*, 1, 15–27.

Hugo, V. (1831). Ce siècle avait deux ans, *Feuilles d'automne*. (This century was two years old). In: *Selected Poems of Victor Hugo: A Bilingual Edition*. Translated by E.H. Blackmore & A.M. Blackmore. Chicago and London: University of Chicago Press, 2001.

Hurtig, M.-C., & Pichevin, M.-F. (Eds.) (1986). *La différence des sexes: Questions de psychologie*. Paris: Editions Tierce.

Kernberg, O. F. (1995). *Love Relations: Normality and Pathology*. New Haven: Yale University Press.

Kessel, J. (1928). *Belle de jour*. Paris: Gallimard.

Lannoy, J.-D. de, & Feyereisen, P. (Eds.) (1996). *L'inceste, un siècle d'inter-pétations*. Paris et Lausanne: Delachaux et Niestlé.

Lanteri-Laura, G. (1978). *Lecture des perversions: Histoire de leur appropriation médicale*. Paris: Masson.

Lanzmann, J. (1976). *Le têtard*. Paris: Laffont.

Laplanche, J. (1993). *Le fourvoiement biologisant de la sexualité chez Freud*. Paris: Synthélabo. Les empêcheurs de penser en rond.

Laqueur, T. (1990). *Making Sex: Body and Gender from the Greeks to Freud*. Cambridge, Mass., & London: Harvard University Press.

Laufer M., & Laufer, E. (1984). *Adolescence and Developmental Breakdown: A Psychoanalytic View*. New Haven and London: Yale University Press.

Legardinier, C. (1997). *La prostitution*. Toulouse: Les Essentiels Milan

Lely, G. (1982). *La vie du Marquis de Sade*. Paris: J. J. Pauvert et Garnier.

Lenoir, F., & Masquelier Y. T. (1997). *Encyclopédie des religions* (2 Vols.). Paris: Bayard.

Leroi-Gourhan, A. (1971). *Les religions de la préhistoire*. Paris: PUF.

LeVay, S. (1993). *The Sexual Brain*. Cambridge: Massachusetts Institute of Technology.

LeVay, S., & Hamer, D. (1994). Pour une composante biologique de l'homosexualité. *Pour la Science*, 201, 30–35.

Lévi-Strauss, C. (1949). *Les structures élémentaires de la parenté* (2nd ed.) Paris: PUF. Paris: Mouton & Co, et Maison des Sciences de l'Homme, 1957. *The Elementary Structures of Kinship (revised edition)*. Translated from the French by J.H. Bell. J. Richard von Sturmer., & R. Needham (Eds.), Boston: Beacon Press, 1969.

Lorenz, K. (1949). *Er redete mit dem Vieh, den Vogeln und den Fischen*. Verlag Wien, Borotha-Schoeler. *King Solomon's Ring: New Light on Animal Ways*. With a foreword by J. Huxley. Trans. by M. Latzke. New York: Routledge, 2002.

Maccoby, E. E, & Jacklin, C. N. (1974). *The Psychology of Sex Differences*. Stanford: Stanford University Press.

Maccoby, E. E. (1990). Gender and relationships, a developmental account. *American Psychologist*, 45, 4, (April 1990), 513–520.

Manassein, M. de, (Ed.) (1995). *De l'égalité entre les sexes*. Paris: Centre National de Documentation Pédagogique.

Manein, P. (1997). Le Gruddhime thevada à Ceylon et dans le pages du sed-Est asiatique. In Lehoir, F. & Masquilier Y.T. *Encyclopéche du religius*, vol. 1, Paris: Bayand, 1021–1029.

Mathieu, N. C. (Ed.) (1985). *L'arraisonnement des femmes*, Paris: Editions de l'Ecole des Hautes Etudes en Sciences Sociales.

McCormack, T. (1988). The censorship of pornography: catharsis or learning? *American Journal of Orthopsychiatry*, 58, 4, 492–504.

McDougall, J. (1993). L'addiction à l'autre: réflexion sur les néo-sexualités et la sexualité addictive. In: A. Fine, A. Le Guen & A. Oppenheimer (Eds.), *Les troubles de la sexualité*. Monographies de la Revue Française de psychanalyse. (pp. 139–157). Paris: PUF.

McDougall, J. (1995). *The Many Faces of Eros*. London: Free Association Books.

Mead, M. (1948). *Male and Female: A Study of Sexes in a Changing World*. New York: William Morrow and Co.

Meyer-Bahlburg Heino, F. L., Migeon, G. D., Gearhart, J. P., Dolezal C., & Wisniewski, A. B. (2004). Attitudes of adult 46, XY intersex persons to clinical management policies. *The Journal of Urology*, 171, (April 2004), 1615–1619.

Moberly, E. R. (1983). *Homosexuality: A New Christian Ethic*. Cambridge, England: J. Clarke.

Money, J. (1955). Hermaphroditism, gender and precocity in hyper-adrena-corticism: Psychologic findings. *Bulletin of the Johns Hopkins Hospital*, 96, 253–264.

Money, J., Hampson, J. G., Hampson, J. L. (1957). Imprinting and the establishment of gender role. A. M. A. *Archives of Neurology and Psychiatry*, 77, 333–336.

Money, J. (1985). The conceptual neutering of gender and the criminalization of sex. *Archives of Sexual Behavior*, 14, 3, 279–290.

Money, J. (1986). *Lovemaps: Clinical Concepts of Sexual/Erotic Health and Pathology, Paraphilia, and Gender Transposition in Childhood, Adolescence, and Maturity*. New York: Irvington.

Money, J. (1988a). *Gay, Straight and In-between: The Sexology of Erotic Orientation*. New York, Oxford: Oxford University Press.

Money, J. (1988b). The ethics of pornography in the era of AIDS. *Journal of Sex and Marital Therapy*, 14, 3, 177–183.

Mouvement du Nid (1987). *Prostitution et Société: Cent questions pour comprendre*. Paris: Mouvement du Nid. *Femmes et mondes*, 79, (October 1997).

Nguyên Du (19 ème siècle), *Kim Vân Kiêu*. Translated into French by Xuân-Phuc & Xuân-Viet. Paris: Gallimard/Unesco, Connaissance de l'Orient, 1961.

Nygren, A. (1930). *Erôs et Agapè: La notion chrétienne de l'amour et ses transformations*. Translated into French by P. Jundt. Paris: Editions Montaigne.

O'Donohue, W., & Caselles, C. E. (1993). Homophobia: conceptual, definitional, and value issues. *Journal of Psychopathology and Behavioral Assessment*, 15, 3, 177–195.

Parat, C. (1995). *L'affect partagé*. Paris: PUF.

Person, E. Spector (1989). *Love and Fateful Encounters*. London: Bloomsbury, New York: Norton & Company.

Person, E. Spector (Ed.) (1997). *On Freud's "A Child is Being Beaten"* with contributions from Jack Novick and Kerry Kelly Novick, Patrick Joseph Mahony, Arnold H. Modell, Leonard Shengold, Marcio de F. Giovanetti, Jean-Michel Quinodoz, Isidoro Berenstein, Rivka R. Eifermann & Marcelo n. Vinar. New Haven and London: Yale University Press.

Pheterson, G. (Ed.) (1989). *A Vindication of the Rights of Whores*. Seattle: The Seal Press.

Pheterson, G. (1996). *The Prostitution Prism*. Amsterdam: Amsterdam University Press.

Réage, P. *Histoire d'O*. An abridged and revised edition including *Le Bonheur dans l'esclavage* by Jean Paulhan. Paris: Jean-Jacques Pauvert, Livre de poche,1997. *The Story of O*. Translated by S. d'Estrée (R. Seaver). Grove Press, 1965.

Reiter, L. (1991). Developmental origins of antihomosexual prejudice in heterosexual men and women. *Clinical Social Work Journal, 19*, 2, 113–175.

Richter-Appelt, H. (2004). Intersexualität und Medizin, Erste Ergebnisse eines Forschungsprojekts. *Zeitschrift für Sexualforschung*, 17, 239–257.

Roiphe, H., & Galenson, E. (1981). *Infantile Origins of Sexual Identity*. New York: International Universities Press.

Sade, Donatien-Alphonse-François, Marquis de (1785). *Les 120 journées de Sodome, ou l'école du libertinage*. Paris:10/18, 1998. *The 120 Days of Sodom and Other Writings*. Compiled and translated by A. Wainhouse & R. Seaver. With essays by S. de Beauvoir & P. Klossowski. New York: Grove Press, 1966.

Saint-Exupéry, Antoine de (1944). Lettre à un otage. In: *Écrits de Guerre, 1939–1944*. Paris: Gallimard, 1982. Letter to a hostage. In: *Wartime Writings 1939–1944*. Trans. by N. Purcell & Fla. Orlando. Harcourt Brace, 1986.

Schaeffer, J. (1997). *Le refus du féminin*. Paris: PUF.

Sergent, B. (1996). *Homosexualité et initiation chez les peuples indo-européens*. Paris: Payot & Rivages. (This volume contains two papers: *L'homosexualité dans la mythologie grecque*. (1984); *L'homosexualité initiatique dans l'Europe ancienne*. (1986). Published by Payot).

Silburn, L. (Ed.) (1997). *Aux sources du bouddhisme*. Paris: Fayard.

Spira, A., & Bajos, N. et le groupe ACSF (1993). *Les comportements sexuels en France*. Paris: La Documentation Française.

Stengers, J., & Van Neck, A. (1984). *Histoire d'une grande peur: la masturbation*. Bruxelles. Editions de l'Université de Bruxelles.

Stoller, R. J. (1968). *Sex and Gender*. vol. 1, (2nd ed.). New York: Science House. *Sex and Gender*. vol. 1, *The development of masculinity and femininity*. New York: Jason Aronson, 1974.

Stoller, R. J. (1970). Pornography and perversion. *Archives of General Psychiatry, 22*, 490–499.

Stoller, R. J. (1975a). *Sex and Gender*, vol. 2. *The Transexual Experiment*. London: The Hogworth Press.

Stoller, R. J. (1975b). *Perversion: The Erotic Form of Hatred*. New York: Pantheon.

Stoller, R. J. (1979). *Sexual Excitement: Dynamics of Erotic Life*. New York: Pantheon.

Stoller, R. J. (1985). *Observing the Erotic Imagination*. New Haven and London: Yale University Press.

Stoller, R. J., & Herdt, G. H. (1990). *Intimate Communications: Erotics and the Study of Culture*. New York, Oxford: Columbia University Press.

Stoller, R. J. (1991a). *Pain & Passion: A Psychoanalyst Explores the World of S & M*. New York and London: Plenum Press.

Stoller, R. J. (1991b). *Porn: Myths for the Twentieth Century*. New Haven and London: Yale University Press.

Stoller, R. J., & Levine I. S. (1993). *Coming Attractions: The Making of an X-rated Video*. New Haven: Yale University Press.

Tap, P. (1985). *Masculin et féminin chez l'enfant*. Toulouse: Privat et Saint-Hyacinthe. Québec: Edisem.

Théry, I. (1997). *Le contrat d'union sociale en question*. Paris: Notes de la Fondation Saint-Simon, Octobre (1997). Published also in: *Esprit*, 1997.

Théry, I. (1998). *Couple, filiation et parenté aujourd'hui: le droit face aux mutations de la famille et de la vie privée*. Paris: Odile Jacob.

Thierry, S. (1997). La "voie du milieu" Selon le bouddhisme. In: Lenoir, F. & Masquelier Y.T, *Encyclopédie des Religions*, vol. 2. Paris: Bayard, 1804–1809.

Tripp, C. A. (1975). *The Homosexual Matrix*. New York: McGraw-Hill.

Vercors (1952). *Les animaux dénaturés*. Paris: Albin Michel.

Vincent, G. (1987). Le corps et l'énigme sexuelle. In: P. Ariès & G. Duby *Histoire de la vie privée* (tome 5), De la première guerre mondiale à nos jours. (pp. 307–389). *A history of private life*. Cambrige, Mass: Bellknap Press of Harvard University Press, 1987–1991.

Vincent, J.-D. (1996). *La chair et le diable*. Paris: Odile Jacob.

Welldon, E. V. (1988). *Mother, Madonna, Whore: The Idealization and Denigration of Motherhood*. New York, London: Guilford Press.

Welzer-Lang, D., Barbosa, O., & Mathieu, L. (1994). *Prostitution: les uns, les unes et les autres*. Paris: Métailié.

Winnicott, D. W. (1956). Primary maternal preoccupation. *Collected papers: Through Paecliatrics to Psycho-Analysis*. London: Tavistock Publications; New York: Basic Books, 1958.

Zavitzianos, G. (1982). The perversion of fetishism in women. *Psychoanalytic Quarterly, 51*, 405–425.

Zhou, J.-N., Hofman, M. A., Gooren, L. J. G., & Swaab, D. F. (1995). A sex difference in the human brain and its relation to transsexuality. *Nature, 377*, n° 6552, 68–70.

Zucker, K. J., Wild, J., Bradley, S. J., & Mowry, C. B. (1993). Physical attractiveness of boys with gender identity disorder. *Archives of Sexual Behavior, 22*, 1, 23–36.

INDEX